VAN AAKEN METHOD

VAN AAKEN METHOD

by Ernst van Aaken

translated by
George Beinhorn

World Publications
P.O. Box 366
Mountain View, CA 94040

CONTENTS

INTRODUCTION

by Tom Sturak

Of the nearly 2000 runners who streamed by during the 1975 Boston Marathon, the 50 women competitors interested Dr. Ernst Van Aaken most. His favorite was the West German, Liane Winter, winner of the Women's International Championship staged the previous fall in his hometown of Waldniel.

Like most of the top German women distance runners, Winter trains by Van Aaken's endurance method. And he knew that "with this tail wind, she would have to arrive around 2:42." As that time approached, he asked that his wheelchair be moved closer to the finish line. At precisely 2:42:24, Liane Winter came across, setting a new world women's mark.

But this record would not stand long, Van Aaken told a companion, because another of his proteges, Christa Vahlensieck, was racing soon in Germany. She, Van Aaken predicted, would run around 2:40-flat. He further stated that if the American, Jacki Hansen, found a favorable course, she would become the first woman to break 2:40. A month later, Vahlensieck recorded 2:40:15. Van Aaken was right. Then, in October 1975, Hansen ran 2:38:19. Van Aaken was right again. He has been called the "Wizard of Waldniel". . .

Without question, Ernst Van Aaken is a most impressive man. Yet he is also enormously likeable. Personages, up close, are not always appealing human beings. And I remember feeling, in the fall of 1971, more awed than excited while en route to Waldniel for a scheduled interview with the legendary "father of LSD" (long, slow distance) training and founder of the Association of Veteran Long Distance Runners, who at age 60 reportedly ran many miles daily and practiced pole vaulting and slept only three hours a night and subsisted on a meager diet . . .

Unforeseen circumstances prevented that meeting, and a year later came the terrible news: While running on the road at night, Van Aaken had been hit by a truck and as a result lost both his legs. This cruel and ironic twist of fate preyed on my expectations when in September 1974 I at last met the man.

But in the flesh Van Aaken radiates an aura of physical strength, intellectual vitality, good humor and lust for life. He may walk unsteadily on artificial legs, using his powerful upper torso (he was first a gymnast in his youth) to propel himself with crutches, but you believe when he says that he is training to compete in a 10-kilometer jogger's run.

Seated in his wheelchair, discoursing brilliantly on the history of women's distance running or on the endurance of migratory birds or on the poetry of Rilke — or behind the wheel of a specially equipped diesel Mercedes (driving with that abandon Germans seem to reserve for the autobahns), he is the compleat man.

Chauffering some women marathoners on an excursion to Dusseldorf, he entertains with songs set to Chopin melodies and elaborates on his working motto: "Run slowly, run daily, drink little, don't eat like a pig." An hour later at a sidewalk cafe, he orders for himself an indecently rich chocolate ice-cream confection. When his startled guests mockingly chide him with his own aphorism, an impish smile flickers across his aristocratic features and he serenely christens the dessert "Marathon Cake."

Cultured and erudite, charming and warm, Van Aaken is also a very funny man. His observations and opinions are characteristically laced with subtle wit. At other times, he can be plain goofy. When an Austrian television reporter asks him to explain why so many women marathoners are attractive, he pontifically deadpans into the camera: "They are beautiful because they run and they run because they are beautiful."

This pervasive sense of humor complements an indomitable determination. Another of his athletic disciples, Olympic marathoner Manfred Steffny, now a journalist, describes a scene that took place in the emergency hospital soon after the amputation of Van Aaken's legs by colleagues "who earlier had given him up for dead":

"The door to Dr. Van Aaken's room is opened. The medical men look up at the ceiling, where the patient is doing gymnastics on a bar which he has had installed above his bed. He does stomach flexions, and, thanks to his strongly developed abdominal muscles, is able to balance horizontally on the bar, which demands a great deal of control over his still painful leg stumps."

Van Aaken himself relishes retelling the story. "They thought," he laughs, "there's an ape, swinging on the chandelier!"

Over the years, Van Aaken has remained aloof of public ridicule and professional neglect while steadfastly refining his radical stances on such matters as the benefits of endurance training, the potential of veteran and women runners, and the rehabilitation of the chronically injured and ill. And dramatic substantiation in recent years of many of his theories has not spoiled the man. His scientist's mind remains open to new data; and he pointedly qualifies even his fondest notions with words to the effect that "this is of course hypothetical" or "we still have much to learn."

Having myself spent considerable time both as an athlete and journalist in the presence of several renowned coaches and sports-medicine practitioners, I find Van Aaken's receptiveness, tolerance and lack of dogmatism particularly refreshing.

Dr. Van Aaken displays wisdom developed over 40 years of scientific investigation and practical application. By his own reckoning, Van Aaken has written some 300 articles and 6000 letters on matters relating to sports medicine and general fitness. He has lectured throughout Europe, in Japan and (most recently) in the United States. He has examined and advised hundreds of runners, including a dozen German national

champions and several Olympic competitors (most notably, Harald Norpoth).

Perhaps most important, he has practiced himself what he preaches. A national collegiate pole vault champion as a heavily-muscled youth, he eventually remodeled his body into that of a typical long-distance runner. Eight times he attempted the marathon before at least finishing one (in 3:17) at the age of 40. When in his 50's, he ran respectable times over 1500 and 5000 meters on the track.

Throughout these years of study and experimentation, Van Aaken has served as a general practitioner in the small, northwest German town of Waldniel. Even when his home is open as headquarters to the scores of athletes, officials and journalists gathered for the International Women's Marathon, Van Aaken continues to see patients.

Stolid townsfolk sit on straight-backed chairs in the lace-curtained dining room and watch with benign curiosity the comings and goings of runners chatting in various languages and loading up on carbohydrates from a table full of open-faced sandwiches and crusty strudel. When his or her turn comes, the ailing burgher passes through the adjoining book-lined den, through Van Aaken's spartanly furnished bedroom and into the small, white-tiled laboratory.

In this modest working cubicle, Van Aaken treats the common ills of his townspeople and the esoteric needs of athletes from the world over. Cluttered with medical paraphernalia and nostrums, its walls are hung with photographs of runners. Lurking on a shelf are liverish-colored plaster models of the hearts of Olympic sprint champion Armin Hary and distance running great Harald Norpoth (his is the larger).

It is in this laboratory, during the wee hours following the

Dr. Van Aaken (shown here in front of his home-office in Waldniel) predicted six months in advance that Jacki Hansen (left) would break 2:40 for the marathon. (Tom Sturak photo)

post-marathon party at which Van Aaken had presided as genial host and amateur photographer, that Dr. Joan Ullyot and I tape a two-hour interview with him (portions appear later in this book). Van Aaken, who (to coin an understatement) thrives on conversation, seems barely warmed up by the time the tapes — and the interviewers — give out at 3:30 a.m. It was too bad, he says, that we could not spend a day or two more at really getting into these matters.

A few hours later, when we return with others to say our bleary-eyed good-byes, he looks fresher than ever in a green and gold Oregon Road Runners Club T-shirt. At the door, he holds up a book and tells us that he has stayed up to study grammar so that the next time we meet he can speak to us in English . . .

We all came together again in Los Angeles in the spring of 1975 during Van Aaken's first visit to the United States. Accompanied by his nephew, Jochen Gossenberger (an accomplished ultra-marathoner), he greeted us: "Hello! I am speaking in English," and then laughed at the joke. His subsequent seminars and lectures were, of course, conducted in German (ably translated by Dr. Ullyot). Even a wizard has limits.

Arriving at the home of his hosts, Dr. Myron and Cisca Shapero, Van Aaken was obviously comforted by its European *gemutlichkeit* (Cisca is Dutch) and pleased to find a piano on which to play his beloved Chopin. But he made clear that he was here "to earn his way." As at home in Waldniel, he continued to work as a restless investigator and staunch advocate of his theories. In preparation for the seminar to be held that very night in the Shapero living room, he declined any morsel of a bountiful and delectable dinner (as an athlete would in the final hours before a race), yet at the same time put all those present at ease with a flow of delightful anecdotes.

In the days following, Van Aaken talked with and examined many athletes (his hosts' living room serving as a "field laboratory"), observed a full training session of the San Fernando Valley Track Club conducted by Laszlo Tabori (who he amazed with precise details of the Hungarian expatriate's

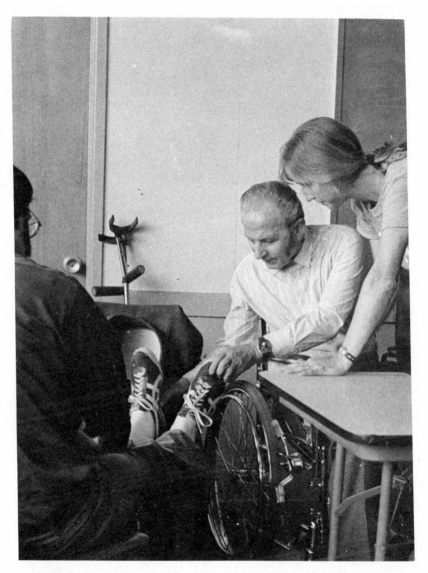

When Dr. Van Aaken was touring the US in 1975, he said he intended to "earn his way." That included both a busy speaking schedule and the examination of injured runners. (OMPhoto)

athletic feats of 20 years earlier) and delivered formal lectures. Despite obviously mounting fatigue and discomfort (he still suffers phantom-limb pains) and a tight schedule (a professional meeting within a day of his return to Germany), Van Aaken agreed to delay his departure for a one-day round-trip to San Diego for a final lecture appearance.

As usual, he enthralled the audience of athletes, doctors, coaches and joggers with his stimulating and controversial ideas on a broad range of subjects: endurance training, dieting and fasting, treatment of injuries, the potential of women as superior ultra-distance runners, a possible explanation for the cause of cancer, conditioning schedules for beginning joggers and heart attack victims, and more.

Here now in this book, for the first time in English, many of the ideas of Ernst Van Aaken are available for close study. They should interest anyone — casual jogger or competitive athlete, overweight housewife or "Type-A" executive — who wants to live a longer and healthier life.

EDITOR'S NOTE

This English-language edition of Ernst Van Aaken's book is only distantly related to the German text from which it was drawn. *Programmed for 100 Years* — the long and, frankly, somewhat rambling and repetitive original — is now the first concise description of the Van Aaken method.

Longtime World Publications staffer George Beinhorn translated, adapted and above all condensed the highly technical German book to make it practical for fitness- and performance-oriented individuals. (The full German version is available from the publisher: Pohl-Celle, Postfach 103, 31 Celle, West Germany.)

We've also added several chapters, both by and about Van Aaken, which previously appeared in *Runner's World* magazine. These are meant to expand on or to clarify important points the doctor makes in his book.

Translator Beinhorn sorted out the essential Van Aaken message, which if it were boiled down to one word would be "endurance" — endurance preferably gained on long runs at moderate paces, endurance expressed in the ability to take in and use oxygen.

Van Aaken says breathing is far more important than eating — more important than anything he could name. Oxygen is the critical life-sustaining element. And his method centers on making more of "the stuff of life" available as a cure and prevention for "the diseases of civilization."

He deals with two apparent extremes in his book: patients

in need of rehabilitation, and high-level competitive runners. But they aren't as far apart as they may seem. He prescribes the same basic method for both of them; only the doses change.

The combination of long runs and low body weight offers abundant health both to patients and athletes. True health, he says, starts with endurance, and from maximum endurance grows maximum performance.

Van Aaken is intent on closing the gap between distance runners and so-called "normal" people by encouraging the inactive ones to start living like runners . . . and by making daily endurance activity the norm instead of the exception it now is.

According to the doctor, "Only the person who runs daily, lives mostly without touching his reserves and who eats little but well will ever become a good runner." Or, for that matter, will acquire the prerequisites of performance — good health.

Part I

Health and Fitness

I
Definition of Health

Health is a constantly changing, multi-faceted sensation with feelings of freshness, endurance, comfort, strength and performance capacity . . . with optimistic, reliable vigor, mental and emotional strength, and a strong life of the soul.

Health consists of a rhythmic rise and fall, a kind of dance of life. It is not static but full of movement, and it has to be re-won, maintained and heightened daily, through the years and decades, up to highest old age. Health is not an average but a heightened norm, an individual's highest achievement. It is the will become visible, the strength of will expressed as durability.

"Normally healthy" today means the weak average person who has made little use of his potential. He often requires a certain amount of illness and catastrophe before he starts trying to climb back up from depths of physical unfitness and emotional depression.

Healthy is not the typical citizen of the 1970's, but the European of the 1940's who was forced by hard times to fight his way through life. Healthy is not one who is accepted into the army, or who gets a passing grade in school physical education classes, or who is relatively free of the diseases of civilization. Rather, healthy is alone he who strives to surpass his own mental and physical boundaries.

Thus, health is not to be separated from above-average ability to perform.

When older runners talk about their above-average health and performance capacity, they usually are told, "Well, of course — you're an athlete." There's a lot of material for discussion in that statement:

1.   The recognition that sports seems to keep one healthy. This everyone realizes, even though shockingly few actually involve themselves in sports.

2.   The non-athlete feels one-upped by the athlete, in a manner of speaking, since athletics demands training which the non-athlete hasn't bothered to apply to himself.

3.   The non-athlete's answer contains a hidden hint that the athlete "has it made" in every respect, since he probably hasn't had the ailments which his conversation partner has experienced.

The general populace is thus convinced that sports keep one healthy. The question then occurs: Which sport keeps a person *really* healthy? Before we can answer that, we have to examine another question: How do doctors define health, and how to athletes define it?

Unfortunately, there is no such thing as an absolutely foolproof standard of health. Electrocardiogram (EKG) readings, for example, have been standardized on many thousands of people who were considered "healthy" but weren't athletically trained. So our picture of a healthy heart is drawn from the lowest common denominator and is a long distance below optimal health.

It's interesting that among competitors in the marathon and 50-kilometer walk at the 1960 Olympics in Rome, 51% had "deviant" EKG curves. Twelve percent had EKG curves that by current standards of the "norm" would be considered pathological.

The EKG is only one method for drawing an approximate picture of health. To get a more accurate picture, we need a number of functional tests. And even when we have this more complete image before us, we have to keep in mind that health is something "flowing," individual, and in many cases it just can't be described in terms of averages.

Health, to give an imprecise definition, is "well-being." It is more precisely characterized by "performance capacity," and a high performance capacity demands true health. If a link in the chain reactions of the organism fails or is weakened, high performance is impossible.

Performance capacity in, for example, weight lifting or figure skating or endurance walking cannot be compared — in fact, performance capacity in the 100-meter dash and the marathon are diametrically opposed.

A fat man, even a cardiac patient, can work himself up to a few seconds of extraordinary speed in a sprint. But does this mean he's healthy? This question hints at the answer we've been looking for: that is, performance capacity in athletic endurance events is the best guarantee of "biological durability" — which can be accepted as a definition of health.

MUSCLE STRENGTH VS. "ORGAN" STRENGTH

The gymnast on the bars, rings, horse, etc. needs strength — pure muscle strength — which he builds mainly by doing exercises on this equipment. The sprinter and the jumper also need strength for fastest possible acceleration, to drive the body forward or upward in fractions of a second.

Muscle strength is the ability to move a mass, a weight. The heart muscle moves a mass too — namely the blood it drives out of its chambers into the arteries with each beat. The strength which makes this work possible is small compared with the biceps strength of a gymnast. But in order to judge heart strength we have to take into account that this organ contracts throughout an entire lifetime, beating about 100,000 times every day. In a single day, the heart does the same work that it would take to lift a 150-pound man to the top of the Eiffel Tower!

All sports and types of work which require pure skeletal-muscle strength, and increase the heart's work by increasing blood pressure within the heart itself and in the arteries, are detrimental to the durability of the organism and to the work of this most important motor, the heart.

This becomes much clearer when we look at what we call "organ strength" — namely the interaction of thousands of chemical reactions in billions of cells. Our organism is material-ized out of a quantity of energy which, if released, would drive the largest ship in the world all the way around the earth. Such powers are bound in the material within us, yet for the maintenance of life as a continuous current in the billions of cells, a pump motor of 1/375th horsepower suffices.

Explosive muscle functions lasting fractions of a second are therefore not as important as the endurance of chemical processes which again and again, like a perpetual clock, renew themselves. They guarantee a durability of about 120 years of life if man did not live in such a hopelessly unbiological fashion, exposed also to hostile environmental influences of absolutely devastating nature. Muscle strength is a tool of the organism and has certain functions in human life. The foundation of the organism, though, is organ strength — especially symbolized by the vital strength of the heart.

THE LOOK OF HEALTH

There's no greater mistake a doctor can make than to diagnose patients' health or illness by their looks, neglecting more precise examination. Naturally, there are outer symptoms of disease which lead the M.D. or layman to a correct diagnosis — yellow jaundice, for instance. But even in such cases, the underlying illness may be quite different than appearances would lead one to expect.

A medical textbook called *The Face of the Coronary Patient* by Schmidt-Voigt contains a photo of a girl who would probably be diagnosed as anemic by any experienced physician. She has reddish-blonde hair, transparently pale cheeks, slightly reddened eyelids, deep shadows around the eyes and conspi-cuously pale lips. The instant diagnosis is completely false. This girl was as "full-blooded" as any healthy adult male.

Equally bad is the case where a healthy person who's proved himself far above the poor average in performance and health is diagnosed ill because of a thin body and face free of fat cheeks and double chin. He is frequently bombarded with advice about what to do for his "condition."

The contemporary German has forgotten that although people looked bad here after the Second World War, they were healthy. Today, the reverse is true, as proved by hundreds of thousands of patients with coronary and circulatory ailments. High blood pressure, for instance, is too often confused with a "good" appearance. And low blood pressure as found in thousands of endurance athletes is diagnosed even by doctors as questionable, if not actually pathological.

Members of the Association of Veteran Distance Runners all over the world have had their share of bad experiences in this respect because of the consensus that a slight figure, pale complexion, and lack of fatty cushions on the face and abdomen are signs of starvation and disease. A number of these athletes have been denied government health certificates and barred from entry in races.

Scarcely has an older man taken up running and put a few kilometers behind him when his wife gets frantic because he no longer looks so "rosy" and his pants no longer fit. His colleagues and friends — particularly the fat ones — tell him in sympathetic tones that "this just cannot be healthy."

The slender figure of Harold Norpoth or Filbert Bayi, among other world-class distance runners, is considered suspect by many people. But what *is* healthy if 13:20 for 5000 meters or 3:32 for 1500 meters isn't?

The glorification of the strong man and the so-called ideal figures of decathletes (who are usually injured in some way or another — and in many cases can be beaten at 1500 meters by sickly looking schoolgirls) have strongly influenced our concepts of health. To look really healthy, a man has to have a lot of muscles and be overweight. But health has nothing to do with mass, and a well-tanned skin after two weeks at the beach is often nothing but varnish over a rotting interior.

The most inconspicuous people are often the toughest, and a good outer appearance very often deceives because it can only hint at possible good internal health.

2
The Basis of Fitness

For health and its cultivation, a person needs two legs and a path for walking and running.

Human beings learn to walk and run in their first year of life. If not, they suffer arrested development. And a person truly needs walking and running when they enter the so-called "fat years" (which unfortunately begin here in Germany between the ages of 14 and 17). This is true because human beings get an increased supply of the most important vital substance — oxygen — only by long walking, mountain climbing, riding a bicycle, cross-country skiing and particularly endurance running. In sedentary living we take about 7-8 liters of air into our lungs per minute, of which about a quarter of a liter is assimilated. If we go for a walk, our oxygen uptake per minute increases to a half-liter. But in light endurance running, done so slowly that one can hold a conversation, about 2-3 liters of oxygen per minute are assimilated from 50-60- liters of air.

We need oxygen in order to chemically change the hydrogen in our organism to water and energy. If a person is very obese, he contains in his fat enormous amounts of hydrogen which he is unable to burn up because in an untrained body oxygen is in too short supply — that is, oxygen cannot be efficiently delivered. To burn up one kilogram of body fat — i.e., to reduce it to water and energy — requires 2000 liters of oxygen, the equivalent to a 100-kilometer run or a walk of even longer distance.

Oxygen is also necessary for the work of the heart, brain and other organs. The brain, for example, is so sensitive to oxygen deficiency that a few seconds without oxygen are sufficient to produce unconsciousness. While a person can survive for many weeks without eating, he can't last five minutes without breathing.

A daily half-hour run delivers enough oxygen to protect a person to some extent from coronary infarct ("heart attack"), circulatory disturbances, obesity and perhaps even against cancer. On the other hand, a deficiency of oxygen may be the cause of the diseases which have particularly plagued us since World War II. In 1947, in conditions of the most extreme privation, coronary infarct was a rarity in my country. In 1958, 38,000 Germans died of this ailment. And by 1970, heart attacks carried off 160,000 − most of them in the age range of 40-55.

We can escape these diseases of civilization only if we do something for our oxygen supply systems, even if it's only a 30-minute endurance run, covering a distance of 5-7 kilometers. It's not a record run of 10 seconds for the 100 meters that will guarantee health, but the long duration of a movement with increased respiration. An hour's run requires 200 or more liters of oxygen. It is not speed and intensity that count, but duration. Every person who is still able to use his legs for forward motion should run and hike or do something similar every day in order to get sufficient oxygen.

It is superfluous to say that a person must also reduce his food intake so that his weight falls well below the so-called norm (a concept of "normal" that has deceived as many laymen as doctors). It is also obvious that cigarettes and sweets as well as fatty foods items in large quantities are to be avoided if a

The concept of running for health has gained enough of a foothold in Germany that the West German president, Walter Scheel, is a participant. (Horst Muller photo)

person is really going to take the maintenance of health seriously.

In general, the modern man whose health means anything at all to him gladly lets himself be talked into all possible measures which supposedly increase health, but which require of him nothing in the way of will-power. Typical are the summer months, when in warm weather thousands suddenly go bathing and lie flat on their backs in the sun for hours at a time, thinking they're doing something really special for their health. It's nonsense to think that tanning one's skin without any kind of physical activity promotes any special kind of health.

The general opinion has also spread that living in a tent for a few days or weeks under conditions somewhat closer to nature will give or guarantee health. If people were truly forced to collect their food in the forest with bow and arrow, and to cover long distances each day on foot, then camping would have a better chance of being a means to health.

Swimming and the other uses of water can be very healthy. But for them to be so, hours of activity requiring real exertion are necessary. Sleeping outdoors doesn't provide one-tenth as much fresh oxygen-containing air as an hour's run.

The only sensible vacation is one that is used to cultivate the basic elements of some endurance sport, whether it's hiking, bicycling, cross-country skiing, forest running or long distance swimming, in order to continue the sport during the remaining 11 months of the year, and to learn during this vacation what it is like to relax after a thorough physical workout. Once this is learned, every day can contain a "vacation" for endurance ability.

DISEASES OF CIVILIZATION

Nowadays, we talk about "diseases of civilization" as something obvious and acceptable, and it's hard not to notice the undertone of rationalization for our own sins against healthy living. We've discovered a whipping boy to take the blame for damage caused by filthy air, water pollution, lack of sunlight, noise damage, the flood of sense stimulation, speed craze in traffic and in occupational life, movement laziness, cigarette addiction, dietary damage and greed, chronic over-fatigue, nervousness, alcoholism, dope addiction and today's most visible catastrophe, coronary infarct and cancer.

All the above-named damages can be boiled down to three basic causes:

1. *Oxygen deficiency.*
2. *Overeating.*
3. *Weakness of will.*

No one would be instantly ready to go without attain-ments of civilization such as industry, telephone and radio, airplanes and autos, central heating, television, preserved foods and modern medications. And in many cases, such renunciation is not necessary because civilization has created the conditions which have made it possible to live longer and better than ever before.

We are not inescapably delivered into the hands of the diseases of civilization, as was formerly the case with smallpox, pestilence and cholera, against which the healthiest person was usually powerless. What can a person do today? Every person could, every day, his whole life long, make a basic rule of doing the following:

In the morning have a warm bath followed by cold shower. Ten minutes of morning gymnastics. Breakfast of no more than 400 calories (menu is individual). Skip the conventional lunch. After work, even if it's late in the evening, an endurance per-formance such as five kilometers of running without getting harried, or a 1000-meter swim, or 15-kilometer bicycle ride, or equivalent exercises which promote endurance and lead to perspiration. Then, after a hot bath or shower, eat dinner.

It's not so important what a person eats, because by the construction of his digestive apparatus he can eat anything. But a person should eat as little as possible and very often make it less than 1600 calories per day. Even if one's work involves hard physical labor and athletic training, he should rarely go over 3000 calories. It is still too little known just how little food a person can get by on. What you breathe is much more important than what you eat.

Hundreds of members of the Association of Veteran Long Distance Runners in the heart-attack-prone group of 40-plus previously were frequently ill. But after they changed their life-style to athletic exertion, they were spared all coronary infarct and became so performance-competent that today it is impossible to imagine what 70- and 80-year-olds in the future will attain.

A shining example: a bank director from the Ruhr industrial area began upon retirement at age 65 to do something for his health, by living according to the above principles. At 70, he ran 10 kilometers on the track in 39:45 and the marathon in 3:13.

ENDURANCE FOR PERFORMANCE

In the 1950's, interval training intended to provoke continuous shortness of breath — oxygen debt — was believed to be the ultimate method for peak-class athletes. But experience since then demonstrated the self-defeating nature of continuous high-speed training and supported my thesis — first published in 1947 — that the basic purpose of training should not be to accustom the body to shortness of breath — at least not as a means of acquiring endurance. The central thought of the endurance method was to continuously increase oxygen uptake capacity by long daily endurance exercise at a moderate pace.

Emil Zatopek — four-time Olympic champion from Czechoslovakia — was the first person in post-war sports to put this idea into practice, in the form of mixed-tempo endurance runs of low intensity, for a total of 35-50 kilometers per day. It is impossible to do this volume of training if one is constantly short of breath. The innovation of Zatopek's training was the unprecedented distance he was running every day.

German coaches and physiologists distorted the very essence of this idea, bringing the uncontrolled speed mania of modern life into athletics in the form of high stresses and the shortest possible recovery breaks. Because some runners actually stood up to this kind of training, bettering Zatopek's times by small margins due to their incomparably better physical endowments, no one bothered to take a hard look at the damage it was inflicting on a whole generation of runners from 1952-64. Athletes who are clearly injured, who are suffering from consistently weak performance, don't generally fall within the observational scope of sports medicine.

Endurance develops most efficiently when one runs in a state of balance between oxygen consumption and oxygen supply. A simple way to gauge proper training speed is to run no faster than one can converse comfortably. The pulse of a runner using the "talk-test" won't rise higher than 150 beats per minute. Professor Hollmann and colleagues proved that the most efficient breathing rate occurs when the pulse is no higher than 130 per minute under conditions of athletic stress. My protege Harald Norpoth had a pulse of 110-150 during 90% of his training mileage, and even during maximal 400-meter runs his heart rate was no higher than 176, measured telemetrically.

The "pure endurance method" I've taught is based on results obtained from about 400 competitive athletes whom I've coached by mail. It guarantees the athlete of any age and of either sex a careful way of exercising for endurance, as a base for sports performances of any other kind.

With this kind of training base, the performance-directed athlete need only add a few tempo runs of moderate intensity at fractions of the racing distance to tune himself for personal maximal performance. Using energy reserves built up over long periods of moderate exercise, he'll have an edge over competitors trained by other methods.

3
Living with Stress

Stress is defined as a severe burden on the organism, with specific sequential reactions. The first person to recognize in stress a general reaction of the entire organism was Dr. Hans Selye, who defined three phases of the stress reaction: (1) alarm; (2) defense reaction of the organism; (3) total exhaustion of counter-regulatory measures. Selye observed in many thousands of animal experiments that stomach ulcers can occur if, for example, the test animal is disturbed day and night by random bell sounds.

Stress for a human being is almost anything he may encounter in his environment which is subjectively associated with certain unpleasant feelings. For example: you have to go to the dentist; the boss calls you into his office to bawl you out; you're facing a difficult school examination; you're an engineer responsible for the success of a difficult construction design; you're an athlete facing your toughest competition after years of preparation. There are thousands of situations in life which can unsettle a person.

Stress and its manifold burdens do not inevitably cause damage — not even in the third state, "exhaustion." People

Air, noise and visual pollution. These are among the stresses pressing in on a runner each day. Dr. Van Aaken thinks running better prepares us to cope with them. (Donald Duke photo)

need certain stimuli in order to learn to switch on their counter-regulatory mechanisms and confront difficult situations in an increasingly tough, calm and sovereign manner.

People who constantly try to avoid the first stage of alarm reaction become addicted to flight from stress and responsibility. In a certain sense, they become incompetent for living. They often end up overindulging in alcohol, tobacco and drugs.

Children should be taught early to confront appropriate stresses and handle them on their own, without assistance. As soon as the child lets go of its mother's hand and explores and conquers the freedom of independent. running, it should be allowed to develop on its own.

This, in fact, should be the rule throughout life. A person who still hangs on mother's apron strings at 20, continually needs father's help and never makes decisions for himself, will probably be helpless before the weighty consequences of even moderately stressful situations.

Would it not be better to practice anti-stress measures from youth, in the form of joyful play, sports and toughening experiences, in order to gain control of one's circulatory system and the emotional reactions demanded by certain risk situations?

It's much too little-known that human beings, created as walkers and runners, can work off the most serious consequences of stress by increasing their oxygen uptake in physical activity — running a few slow miles for recovery after a hard day's work for instance, however paradoxical that may sound to the uninitiated. The experienced runner knows he recovers best from even highly stressful situations of the day by the comfortable exertion of easy running, after which he is free to enjoy his evening hours in a well-balanced mood.

Five conditions are necessary to keep the mind fit and stress-resistant:

1. *Practice endurance daily.*
2. *Avoid overweight, and eat and drink moderately.*
3. *Exercise muscle strength and coordination.*

4. Exercise will-power daily.

5. Don't let your mind go to seed.

A person who's practiced anti-stress discipline for years on end ought to be more equal to today's great wave of sense overstimulation and environmental dangers.

STRESS OF SPORT

The average doctor gives his okay to sports, but with the condition that it "shouldn't be overdone." Yet most of these athletic laypeople and medical experts are not clear as to the precise limits which ought to be drawn.

The human organism is not made in such a way that it can survive near-maximal efforts for hours on end. Rather, the body reaches a certain upper limit on oxygen debt, heart rate, breathlessness and performance capacity of the musculature at near-maximal stresses of 50 seconds duration. Translated into practical terms, this means that a 400-meter run can produce total exhaustion in 50 seconds.

"Too much" in athletic training is, then, a matter of the intensity of the stresses involved, and not of the duration. A cyclist, swimmer, mountain climber, Nordic skier, long-distance runner, soccer player or gymnast can exercise for hours without "overdoing it" if he chooses a tempo that's comfortably suited to him. This will be a pace which guarantees a liberal supply of oxygen through breathing, does not make the pulse rise over 130 and, in biochemical terms, doesn't lead to the accumulation of lactic acid.

Even a 100-kilometer run, done at a comfortable pace with sufficient rest intervals, may be no more than an agreeable test while a 400-meter race at top speed — in spite of its short duration — can lead to exhaustion with certain damaging consequences. A person who trains daily at a pace that guarantees a balance of oxygen consumption and carbon dioxide elimination can never do "too much."

"Too much" is when the intensity of the exercise is increased and continued to such an extent that the by-products of fatigue begin to accumulate, leading finally to a burned-out state, loss of enthusiasm, and a series of steadily-falling performances.

Athletes are easily enthused and led into hard training which has as its motto, "If it hurts, it must be doing some good." This kind of training, which satisfies the masochistic urges of many athletes, does not build reserves or improve performances, but rather destroys a person's sense of the playful joy of training and sports.

Part 2

Oxygen and Endurance

4

The Breath of Life

Energy is required in all processes of life, and energy is produced in the cells almost exclusively by chemical reactions which consume oxygen.

We humans are land animals living in a sea of air. I might remark in this connection that swimming is an artificial invention of man which he can learn as part of his physiological bag of tricks. But man is, compared to the fishes and other marine animals, a bungler — and to a certain extent he is only fooling himself when he practices swimming as a sport. The physical system which he's developed for life on land is carried by the buoyancy of water and thus made less suitable for movement on land. This is particularly true of the legs — because man is a running animal.

Water sports and swimming can serve admirably for therapy in cases of paralysis and impaired movement of the joints. But to specialize in these movements goes against the nature of a land animal.

I am not an opponent of swimming. But people have to be taught again which is their natural life-zone. The human life-zone is the land. Movement on land strongly promotes oxygen uptake and makes the organs of the body more fit on an endurance basis. Land movement is important biologically for man, and is incomparably effective for building health.

Man has been living in the years since shortly after WWI in a hopelessly unbiological fashion — this applies even to certain practices in sports — and only an increased supply of oxygen for all his many billions of cells can save him. As long as mankind doesn't understand the importance of oxygen as an elixir of life, so long will diseases of civilization continue to increase. Medications and physical methods of treatment will prove ineffective if they bypass the true path to health — which is the promotion of oxygen supply. Oxygen must be acquired, according to thermodynamic laws, by the application of effort, since without effort no energy is produced.

The problem confronting every organism living on land consists of bringing oxygen from the environment into the living cell. A principle of physics is involved: substances tend to migrate from regions of greater concentration to regions of less concentration. Thus, oxygen from the air, where its concentration is 21%, passes into the interior of the cell, where its concentration as free molecular oxygen is nil.

The larger and heavier an organism is, the more cells there are in its interior. So their danger of dying from oxygen deficiency is increased by the acquisition of inactive body weight — of mass. Where fat mass is great, excess hydrogen places excessive demands on the already small quantities of oxygen that can be delivered. This causes a number of pathological effects.

EFFECTIVE BREATHING

The maximal volume of our lungs is on the average about 6-7 liters. The air in the lungs at any one time is not sufficient to maintain life because its oxygen is completely used up after a very few minutes. It is therefore necessary to continually renew this air by breathing, and so a person, depending on body size, must take in 6-10 liters of air per minute, in 12-20 breaths.

Respiration may be subordinate to our will — we can practice deep inhalation and exhalation or hold our breath for minutes at a time. But the most important control of respiration is beyond the scope of will, and goes on automatically in the organism. When we sleep or are busy working, respiration follows a steady rhythm in depth and breaths per minute, corresponding to the body's need for oxygen.

Our involuntary breathing rate depends on the concentration of carbon dioxide in the lung's bronchioles. When carbon dioxide rises above the norm, respiration becomes quicker and deeper. If the concentration sinks, respiration is slow and very shallow. Carbon dioxide concentration in the lungs thus controls our respiration against our will. Even if with great will-power a person holds his breath to the point of unconsciousness, this involuntary mechanism again brings things back to order. The opposite is also possible — you can get dizzy from too much oxygen, by willfully breathing in and out very rapidly, exhaling every last bit of carbon dioxide and disturbing normal circulation. When you relax, you find you'll stop breathing completely for a few seconds. In normal breathing at rest, we use up, as mentioned earlier, 6-10 liters of air and take about 150-250 cubic centimeters of oxygen into our systems every minute. If we go for a walk, oxygen uptake rises to a half-liter of oxygen per minute with a minute-volume of air of 15 liters or so. A simple stroll is not enough to keep the organism healthy, because truly health-promoting processes begin only when 40 liters of air per minute are supplied, containing about 1.5-2.0 liters of oxygen. Beyond this range — in harder endurance exertion when 80 or more liters of air are being pumped with 4-5 liters of oxygen — respiration becomes choked and maximally taxed and reserves are called up. This leads, sooner or later, to exhaustion.

Breathing exercises have little effect on the respiration figures and can at most teach proper breathing technique. Only by physical endurance exertion can more than 10 times as much oxygen be brought in through the lungs than in the resting state. A person's health and performance capacity depend predominantly on his going considerably beyond the normal resting figures for respiration, thereby increasing oxygen supplying capacity.

Oxygen uptake of a quarter-liter per minute at rest can be increased in a trained person to five liters, or 20 times the resting value. But it's generally sufficient to practice 10-fold oxygen supply frequently and for long periods at a time. This is in the form of endurance exercise, particularly endurance running during which the person must be able to hold a conversation and the pulse should not rise beyond the 130-150 range. The breathing *rate* remains about the same in proper physical endurance work as at rest, while breathing *volume* uniformly rises. Physical rest produces only a slight upward swing of renewed vitality, while endurance performance brings a mighty, bubbling spring of life.

5

Protection from Cancer

from Leichtathletik Magazine

This article originally appeared in the German magazine Leichtathletik and was reprinted in Runner's World, May 1971.

"Statistical proof of a possible prevention of cancer through years-long, increased endurance functioning of biological oxidation, with a view of the final cause of cancer." That is the somewhat complicated title of a medical-scientific work which Ernst Van Aaken, M.D., recently published. In plain English, the title of this work might be: "Does slow endurance running, continued over many years, protect a person from cancer?" This is an interesting topic, and it is no coincidence that Dr. Van Aaken is the person dealing with it since, as is well known, he is the German prophet of long running training at a pace where no oxygen debt is acquired.

Dr. Van Aaken had stated in a previous paper that among members of the Association of Veteran Long Distance Runners there had been no reported case of cancer. Professor Otto Warburg, a noted cancer researcher, was not satisfied. He asked for statistical proof. Dr. Van Aaken then sent a questionnaire to about 1000 senior (over-40) distance runners all over the world.

Van Aaken theorizes that men in the most cancer-prone age groups are protected because they regularly take in great amounts of oxygen. These 75-year-olds practice the prescription.

Four-hundred fifty-four questionnaires were returned to him; some had been answered with the backing of family doctors or specialists. The distance men were between 40 and 89 years old; the average age was 53.8. They had been active in sports for an average of 32.4 years – in running, mostly by the endurance method, for 19.6 years. The seniors who completed the questionnaire didn't form a "physical elite." Dr. Van Aaken reports that seven of them have already had a heart attack, and 74 had severe circulatory disturbances before they began long distance training. Only two of the 74 are still suffering from these ailments. The runners have been through other diseases ranging from bronchitis to dysentery or malaria, and have had operations of various kinds.

"The most important result of the whole questionnaire project was, however," states Dr. Van Aaken, "that all together only four cases of tumor formation were determined." None of these cases resulted in death. One was really questionable. Two of the three other distance men feel healthy again, among them a 71-year-old physician who was originally very depressed but now is again running five kilometers daily.

Dr. Van Aaken compared the evaluation of the 454 questionnaires from senior runners with the same number of 40-90-year-old patients in his practice. This group were non-athletes, some were heavy smokers, some alcoholics, every fifth person was heavily overweight. Among them, Dr. Van Aaken found 19 verified and 10 probable cases of carcinoma (cancerous tumors).

"The comparison of the two groups: 454 fit senior runners with four tumors = 0.89%; 454 men from a country practice between 40 and 90 years of age with 29 tumors = 6.4%, which can serve as clear proof that a healthy way of living, continued for years, with fasting, non-smoking and daily running training does not only give extensive protection from cancerous diseases, but preserves a performance capacity on into high old age which even some (younger) trained athletes cannot show."

Van Aaken offers a possible explanation: "Otto Warburg has shown experimentally that healthy mouse cells, under conditions of 30% decrease in oxygen pressure, degenerate irreversibly into cancer cells within 48 hours.

"Endurance training, carried on at a moderate pace with optimal breathing efficiency, is because of its optimal provision of oxygen to all 60 billion cells of the organism the best guarantee of prevention of cancer in certain forms which may depend on a throttling of the oxygen supply."

The opinion he has distilled from his research, "that an optimal running training with eightfold increase in the endurance function of the biological oxidation process, carried on for years, prevents cancer with 99% certainty." If this is true, slow endurance running training will take on a heightened significance for the maintenance of health.

6
Miles and Miles of Heart

The greatest importance of the heart and circulatory system is in what they carry — namely blood. The most important function of the blood is to transport oxygen.

The heart is a hollow muscle which can hold a certain quantity of blood and which by contracting drives this blood into the arteries for distribution to the body cells. The average volume of this hollow muscle in a healthy adult who has not been doing endurance sports is 700 cubic centimeters.

The heart of the fit endurance athlete has a greater internal volume, about 900-1400 cc. With each beat under working stresses, it drives nearly 10 times as much blood into the system as at rest. The athlete's heart beats not 72 times per minute like the average healthy person's, but usually 60 or fewer — and as few as 30 in some exceptional cases. The endurance athlete's blood pressure and pigment quantities are greater than average, allowing him to take in and transport more oxygen. The endurance-trained person's blood is more fluid and thus more easily driven through his arteries, which are more elastic than the average.

The heart is a "mini-motor" — marvelous not for what it does with each individual beat, but for its durability. The heart is made for endurance performance, not for peak performance over short time periods. The human heart is the best endurance muscle of all. Man is, by the nature of his own heart, not suited for sprint running at distances of 100, 200 and 400 meters. As a land animal he is definitely a long-distance runner, similar to the horse. Indeed, man is even in a position to run longer than a horse, because horses stop running when their muscles become tired, while man can continue running to total exhaustion by virtue of the strength of his mind and will. No animal would ever do this given a free choice.

The story is told of the ancient Incas that a royal messenger ran nearly 1000 kilometers in five days. If he had run 10 hours each day and rested 14 hours he would have had to cover five kilometers every 15 minutes. More likely, this runner did repetitive runs with short pauses, running all day at an easy, slow pace and taking recovery breaks from time to time. If he ran 20 hours a day and spent the other four hours in recovery pauses, this would mean running every 5000 meters in 30 minutes, or 10 kilometers an hour. There do exist runners today, trained by the endurance method, who are capable of similar performances. For example, on June 4, 1970, the longest non-stop walking race in the world went from Strasbourg to Paris, 510 kilometers. The winner was 36-year-old Samuel Zaugg, in about 70 hours.

Endurance performance is founded on the design of the heart, because the heart muscle is always excellently supplied with oxygen and never incurs an oxygen debt. Between the fibers of its muscles are many millions of mitochondria, the respiratory factories of the cell. A single cell of trained heart muscle contains 3000-4000 mitochondria. The endurance abilities of the heart muscle depend directly on the number of respiratory factories it contains.

LARGE MOTOR, LIGHT FRAME

Medical science once considered any heart that was enlarged to be pathological, since people who had died from heart disease were consistently found to have damaged hearts which were unusually large. Then in 1920, the Swedish doctor Henschen decided to test the best racers in the Vasa ski run of 90 kilometers, since these athletes had proved their coronary health in performance. Surprisingly for contemporary medical

science, the hearts of the highest placers were all enlarged. Decades later, professional cycle racers and marathon runners were likewise found to have enlarged hearts but had nevertheless proved their coronary health in great performances. Over the last 30 years, these findings have been repeatedly confirmed — with the reservation that enlargement of the heart should not continue without limit, but can only be characterized as healthy as long as performance capacity increases at a rate parallel with heart enlargement, as judged by racing times, etc.

Only in sports with prolonged movement of moderate intensity does the heart develop in endurance and volume. Thus, Olympic 100-meter champion at Rome, Armin Hary of Germany, had the heart of a child — only 606 cubic centimeters in volume, though he had powerfully developed driving muscles in his legs. A 100-meter run at world-class level is not won with the heart but with strong legs and fast nerve reactions. Middle-distance runners have a somewhat larger heart than the average man who has never done sports, namely, 900 cc. Only the long distance runners — especially marathon runners — or athletes in other sports which require training of longer than an hour a day, will have heart enlargement up to 1000 cc. as a gradual result of their specific training.

If the endurance athlete's body weight remains low, 10-20% under the so-called norm, the result is a favorable relationship between the small mass of the body and the great motor performance of such a large heart. This factor is particularly important for long distance running performance ability, and for general durability and longevity. If, for example, we have a massive decathlete or shotputter of 100-kilogram body weight, with good heart volume of 1000 cc., we could divide that 1000 cc. by 100 kg. for a factor of 10. This factor is too small to permit us to call the person in question truly

Eva-Marie Westphal, a German who trains by the Van Aaken principles, has run the fastest marathon for a woman in her 50s. Her time: 3:23. (Horst Muller photo)

enduring. But if the athlete weighs only 50 kilos, with a heart volume of 1000 cc., the endurance factor would be 20, which would be just as high as for the world's best distance runners.

Russian marathoner and European champion in 1958, Popov, weighed 50 kilos and had a heart volume of 1200 cc., which gave a factor of 24 – the highest figure of this kind to have been measured to date. German world-class runner Harald Norpoth, who weighs about 58 kilos, had a heart volume of 1243 cc. eight weeks before his second-place finish in the Olympic 5000-meter race at Tokyo. His factor was 21.4. However, an exemplary world-class middle-distance runner like Paul Schmidt, fourth-place finisher in the 800 meters at the Rome Olympics, had a factor of only 13.9.

Developing endurance, then, is a matter of keeping body weight as low as possible, while increasing heart strength as expressed in a large heart volume and low blood pressure and low pulse frequency. This assures optimal blood transport and circulation to supply the 60 billion cells of the body with a continuously abundant supply of oxygen.

The faster the heart rate, the less efficient is the filling of the ventricles and their recovery time after contraction. Above a pulse rate of about 162-168, the amount of blood pumped out with each heart beat decreases and the reserve blood in the ventricular reserves can no longer be economically used at all. For these reasons and many other considerations, it becomes clear that the German interval training system with high stress loads and pulse rates of 180 plus shortest recovery pauses was like cracking the whip over the reluctant heart.

Such interval training is a form of "destructive testing," while endurance training should be hours of easy playing. Optimal oxygen uptake at a heart rate of 130, an increased pumping capacity of the heart per beat to about 110 cc. and blood pressure no higher than 200 mm. of mercury are the characteristics of biologically sane training, which can be done for hours daily. This is the way it's done in modern training in most sports, and this is what makes contemporary performances possible.

Also, it is being recognized more and more that slow endurance running with walking breaks is the best prevention for heart and circulatory disease. It is certain, especially in view of my experiences with older long distance runners of 40-90 years of age from all over the world, that slow running at a pace which makes for optimal oxygen supply, plus weight loss and reduction of body fat, are the one sure path to escaping the fate of our innumerable heart and circulatory patients.

7
The Road to Recovery

Nearly every peak-class athlete who has turned up at my medical office during the last 30 years — and there have been nearly 1000 — has told me that other doctors invariably prescribe the path of least resistance for athletic injuries. The doctor orders rest and recuperation, which is hardly what the athlete wants, since he's only trying to find out how he can continue to work, train and race *in spite of* his injury. But since this kind of treatment doesn't get written into medical textbooks, the immediate prescription is usually a layoff.

An eight-time German national long distance running champion was radiologically diagnosed as suffering from lung ailment. Fortunately for him, only his personal physician and I had made the diagnosis. He continued his customary training on my advice because, in principle, stimulation of the respiratory functions by long distance running ought to better promote healing in a diseased lung than a rest cure with rising weight. Otherwise, we'd have to train our Olympic team's performance capacities with bed rest and good food. This runner won the 5000-meter bronze medal at the Helsinki Olympics two years later.

Another young athlete, who'd already been ordered into a tuberculosis sanatorium by public health authorities, was found by me to be healthy after X-ray examination. Three months later, he won the German age-group 400-meter title. Even tubercular patients have to go on breathing every minute of their lives, and their ability to do so gets worse when they're subjected to rest cures and inactivity. It's not tuberculosis that frequently ruins such "borderline cases," but inappropriate inactivity — the prescriptions and prohibitions which effectively run counter to the patient's constitutional rights.

I don't want by these observations to spread distrust of physicians, but only to point out that patients with certain ailments can be brought to ruin through inactivity. When they break doctor's orders, they actually improve.

Around 1950, no one would have dared take bed-ridden heart patients out after six days to begin easy running; if anything had happened, the physician would certainly have been jailed for malpractice. But nowadays we read every week in medical journals articles testifying to increasing advocacy of active convalescence for coronary patients.

To my knowledge, Professor Gottheiner of Israel was one of the first to rehabilitate coronary infarct patients with step-by-step, graduated training. But in Germany, most clinics are too timid to advocate running, the most natural form of oxygen-promoting activity for heart patients — even though physiology has proved that even at a pulse rate as low as 120 beats per minute eight times as much oxygen is assimilated as in the resting state. This promotes rapid healing.

A 38-year-old with diagnosed infarct was treated gently for a year, declared unfit for work for the entire period. He began training under my guidance, jogging only 350 meters while a conversation was maintained. After 350 meters, a 50-meter walking break was taken, then he ran 350 meters, etc. On this training, the "occupationally disabled" patient progressed in just five months to the point where he ran a marathon, finishing in astonishingly fresh condition with a time of 3:44.

"IRREGULARITIES"

About 8% of the best athletes in the section of Germany where I serve as a track and field physician have been erroneously diagnosed as having coronary disease in the last 10 years, and in many cases have been so diagnosed by a number of specialists.

Because of its absurdity, I give here a particularly crass example. A nine-year-old school girl was told she couldn't swim because of a presumed coronary irregularity, diagnosed by EKG. She was one of the best swimmers in her age-group. Medical examination revealed the extraordinary performance capacity of this child. No pathology was discovered by X-ray examination. After three months of training she was German national schoolgirl champion in the 100-meter breast stroke, and now she's a hope for the next Olympics.

The medical profession, trained on sick people and scarcely aware of data from sports physiology, is inclined to look at the peak-class performer with mistrust. Thus, a presumed sufferer from coronary disease who'd previously run 10,000 meters in 31 minutes was shocked to discover at a pre-race physical that he needed an immediate six-week layoff with complete bed-rest. I examined him and found his resting pulse to be 36; after a 10,000-meter run, it dropped to 48 in just one minute. Two years later, the "patient" won the German national marathon title.

Therefore, I wonder about the standards of the medical profession. Is a person healthy if, amid moans and groans, he can survive 20 deep knee bends for a life insurance examiner and if his pulse returns to "normal" after two minutes? Or is a runner sick who can run 10,000 meters and have his pulse drop to 48 within a minute?

increasing muscle size and by practicing oxygen debt.

Interval training with relatively high stresses causes increased tension in the muscles, with consequent poor circulation while running.

Interval training increases the diameter of muscle fibers, while the area of oxygen diffusion becomes proportionately less favorable.

Interval training produces an increase in the heart's size in a short time by high stress intensity.

Interval training produces regulative heart expansion and hypertrophy (abnormal enlargement).

Interval training runs the danger of overdoses and the application of stimuli that exceed what is optimal.

Interval training, because of its many repetitions, applies stimuli which are not optimally related in quantity to the momentary performance capacity of the organism.

Interval training provokes lactic and pyruvic acid formation.

oxygen uptake at the endurance performance boundary) to favorably affect endurance and heart quotients, which make possible higher average running speeds.

In endurance training at a slow pace, in a "steady state" at the endurance performance boundary, circulation remains nearly optimal.

Endurance training increases the aerobic capacity of muscle fibers and the number of capillaries. Oxygen supply to the muscle fibers improves because of, among other things, a slowing of blood flow speed and high oxygen utilization.

Endurance training produces an increase in heart volume over a long period (2-6 years) and with low stress intensity.

Endurance training tries to improve running performance by avoiding training for muscle strength and by increasing enzyme activity of the entire musculature.

Because it involves a spreading out of stresses over a longer time period, endurance training does not as easily involve overdoses, and it produces normal optimal stimuli.

Endurance training applies a dosage of stimuli which is always in a proper relationship to performance capacity.

Endurance training avoids as far as possible all formation of lactic and pyruvic acids, particularly during the base training period of long runs.

Interval training attempts to increase the activity of the enzymes of glycolysis.

Endurance training attempts to increase the activity of the enzymes of biological oxidation.

Interval training works with heart rates of from 150-200.

Endurance training works with endurance pulse rates of 150 and less.

In interval training, the exhausted cell ejects potassium into the serum, completely exhausting the cell's potassium energy reserves.

In endurance training, the cell eliminates predominantly sodium and water, and assimilates potassium, thus increasing its energy potential.

In interval training, there is a hypothetical discharge of myoglobin during continuous critical stresses.

Endurance training increases the amount of hemoglobin and myoglobin, especially in altitude training.

Interval training seeks the leg muscles desirable for sprinting, so as to make the runner faster at all distances.

Endurance training seeks a marathon runner's legs, which have five times the endurance of a sprinter's, in order to produce speed at all distances beyond 400 meters.

Interval training provokes exponential increases in energy consumption and poor efficiency during relatively anaerobic metabolism.

Endurance training reveals a linear increase in energy consumption with increasing time and distance, and thus economical efficiency.

Interval training continually practices running speeds not required for one's specialized racing distance.

Endurance training prefers for its tempo runs running speeds at one's specific racing speed.

Interval training, because of its too intense and too frequent stresses, causes anaerobic fatigue by-products to accumulate — which in the final analysis may interfere with the speed the runner is trying to develop.

Endurance training avoids fatigue by-products and endurance-trained athletes are often able to finish faster than interval-trained runners because of their endurance reserves.

Emil Zatopek (left) used "classical interval training"—rather slow repetitions with jogging in between, which allowed him to go much farther than otherwise possible.

9
How Much? How Fast?

Endurance training has created runners who can begin their burst ("finishing kicks") early and accelerate for a 400-, 600- or 800-meter final effort. Peter Snell, the slowest sprinter of the six finalists in the 800 meters at the Rome Olympics, won his race by bursting over the last 100 meters, a result of his still-fresh reserves. Harald Norpoth ended a 5000-meter run in 1965 with a 600-meter burst in 1:19.8, a time which middle-distance runners of the interval era could scarcely have matched in an 800-meter run.

My own marathon training from 1947-57 showed me that I was faster at all racing distances — even at 400 meters — when I'd acquired endurance. There must, therefore, be an optimal training speed and training distance for every racing distance. The empirically discovered criterion of good oxygen supply corresponded to a pace in training at which a person could still conduct an uninterrupted conversation. The approximate boundary for pulse frequency was about 120-130 per minute.

The daily mileage found ideal for each racing distance was, in average values:

Race	Training*
400 meters	6 kilometers
800 meters	10 kilometers
1500 meters	15 kilometers
3000 meters	20 kilometers
5000 meters	25 kilometers

10,000 meters	30 kilometers
Marathon	40 kilometers

*Depending on constitution, age, sex, etc., the distances are shortened or lengthened, breaks introduced or continuous running used. Breathlessness is avoided during this long training.

Tempo runs were added to the basic endurance work, and later reduced until the formula was established that the runner's race pace should be practiced year-round after each day's training run, depending on his present condition and health. Sprint intervals of 50 meters were adopted from New Zealand training because theoretically no oxygen debt of large proportions can occur during this kind of work. They are used in my training only on occasion, and only as a final polish.

The acquisition of long-distance speed does not demand continuous near-maximal provocation of energy expenditures. Rather, there must be a threshold where energy expenditure and continuous formation of energy are balanced in a way that continuation of the process increases one's energy "capital."

HOW MUCH SPEED?

A difficult problem in the preparation of middle- and long-distance runners is to decide whether tempo runs can be further de-emphasized as compared with their predominance in interval training, or whether a runner can get along without any tempo runs. It has been my frequent observation that peak-class runners can run times on the roads in winter and spring — on no tempo runs at all — which they were unable to run previously on even the hardest kind of tempo work.

The improvement of the 5000-meter world record from 14:20 in 1936 to 13:13 in 1972 must be credited almost entirely to the increase in moderate-paced training mileage, and to a decreasing emphasis on high-intensity interval training with short pauses. One example of what has happened is German runner Siegfried Herrmann. Trained on frequent days of 30 x 200 meters, Herrmann ran the 5000 in about 14:10 in 1960. In 1966, after switching to an endurance-based system, he suddenly ran 13:30.

The endurance training method for middle and long distance runners can be expressed in a few simple rules, many of which I've alluded to earlier:

● *Run daily, run slowly, with creative walking breaks.*

● *Run many miles, many times your racing distance if you are a track runner; up to and often beyond if you are a long-distance runner. Do tempo running only at fractions of your racing distance.*

●. *Run no faster during tempo runs than you would in a race.*

● *Bring your weight down 10-20% under the so-called norm and live athletically — i.e., don't smoke, drink little or no alcohol, and eat moderately.*

● *Consider that breathing is more important than eating, and that continuous breathlessness in training exhausts you and destroys your reserves.*

After about two years of base training — endurance running only — middle and long distance runners can train along the following lines (remember that these are only examples; individual runners will vary):

1. 10 x 350-meter jog with 50-meter walking pauses (total 4000 meters), followed by 2000 meters two minutes slower than one's best possible time. Then 5 x 300 meters, and another 2000 meters, 1½ minutes slower than one's best time, etc. From the third month of training on, do a tempo run of 600 meters about 10 seconds slower than your best possible time. Tempo runs can be done also at 800 and 1000 meters, at a corresponding pace.

2. 10 x 350-meter jog with 50-meter walking breaks, then 5000-meter run at a pace four minutes slower than one's best time, followed by a tempo run as described above.

3. Open-country run by the interval principle, 10-30 kilometers total distance — i.e., either 2000-meter runs at a pace two minutes slower than one's best time and walking breaks of 3-5 minutes, or 3000-meter runs at a pace 3-4 minutes slower than one's best time with similar walking breaks. Follow with

one or two tempo runs at 400 to 600 meters on the track with walking and jogging breaks.

4. Continuous cross-country or road run of 10-20 kilometers on varied terrain — but with no uphill acceleration — at a "conventional" pace.

5. Mixture of open-country and track running (the latter consisting of two tempo runs and, if indicated, a time trial at one's racing distance or a fraction thereof).

6. This workout is especially useful after hard running the day before or in cases of tendon or muscle injury which prevent longer, continuous running: 25-50 x 350-meter jog with 50-meter walking breaks (total: 10-20 kilometers) on the infield of the track.

"Endurance mileage" is related to "tempo mileage" in a ratio of about 20:1. As mentioned earlier, total training distances are increased or shortened to correspond with one's preferred racing distance.

Anyone can estimate the best stress levels for their tempo runs from their best racing times. For example, a 15-minute 5000-meter runner will run 1000 meters in three minutes, a 2:00 800-meter runner can do 200 in 30 seconds, etc. The calculated times for tempo sections of a longer run are estimated by feeling, without a stopwatch, after some initial practice.

SOMETHING EXTRA

Oxygen economy can only be improved if each morning, after 10 minutes of warmup exercises, the runner slowly jogs 5-10 kilometers on the road or a cross-country course. At the beginning or end of the week everyone takes their longest training run. The 800-meter specialist does 20-25 kilometers, the marathon runner 40 kilometers and occasionally 60, 80 or 100 kilometers. During the first years of training such distances will have to be run with a walking break every 2-5 kilometers.

The runner in the middle and long distances should learn to fast again, and run best with a certain feeling of hunger. Digestive work shortly before and during a run wastes energy.

The runner must have occasional training days when he eats no food at all, so as to learn to live solely off his own stored body substances.

The runner can eat anything that tastes good to him, and that is offered by his environment, but he should not eat more than 2000 calories per day. About 50 grams per day of high-quality protein is important, since the endurance athlete is an "enzyme athlete" and the enzymes are high-quality protein bodies which are insufficiently supplied by all-raw and similar diets.

The leading role given carbohydrates in recent years should be very much de-emphasized. It is recommended only in foods like bread, potatoes, rice, honey and fruit. No more than 40 grams of fat should be eaten per day, including 15 grams of butter and 25 grams of oils rich in linoleic acid, as found in good-quality margarines. The protein requirement of the runner is met with two eggs per day and 200 grams of lean meat.

Sleep is an individual matter, but in general people more often sleep too much than too little.

Many diseases and indispositions — particularly muscle tendon and joint problems — can be combatted with warmup exercise and hot baths. Movement therapy is the most important medicine in handling runners' ailments, except in the case of broken bones. If ligaments, tendons and muscles of the leg are not severely injured, training on a racing bicycle will be possible — and far better than a total layoff.

10

Pauses that Refresh

by Joe Henderson

Dr. Van Aaken has provided much of the scientific rationale behind Joe Henderson's "LSD" (long, slow distance) ideas. The author of Run Gently, Run Long wrote of Van Aaken in the July 1975 Runner's World.

Dr. Ernst Van Aaken has been my conscience for a long time. I'd known about him, quoted and misquoted him for 15 years, but never met him or understood him until 1975.

I was a high school senior in 1960 when *Track and Field News* offered a new publication — a technical quarterly filled with training advice. It was to be edited by my absentee coach, Fred Wilt, and he was to introduce me to this Dr. Van Aaken from Germany.

Prophetically, Van Aaken had the first article in the first issue of *Track Technique*. I skimmed the first paragraph of "Speed or Endurance Training?" — which didn't seem to have much to do with me — and hurried into the second, where the doctor started talking numbers and schedules.

Now I'm rereading his introduction: "According to my observations, it is just children who are born long distance runners. Any healthy boy or girl is able to run as much as three miles at a moderate pace. The play of children is nothing more than a long distance run, because in a couple of hours of play they cover many kilometers with several hundred pauses. The play of children is a primal form of interval training."

In 1960, I thought I was no longer a child and should not

run like one. My running was no longer playful, and I was into a more serious kind of interval work.

I followed what I imagined to be the teaching of Mihaly Igloi. In the early '60s, his runners were tops and I blindly imitated them. This broke me down. I'd use slow running to recover, then would run myself into another breakdown, again and again. The biggest breakdown came in 1966, when I decided to make all my running "recovery" running.

Dr. Van Aaken was there that year, reminding me what had happened: "The continual practicing of high speed, beyond racing speed, is uneconomical and leads to decreases in reserves." Good running, he said, involves little more than staying fresh — never getting really tired or sore. If you do get that way, then take plenty of time to recover.

By 1970, I'd embraced Ernst Van Aaken as my personal guru and was writing about him. I used him to support my LSD ideas, and shut out what I didn't want to hear.

For instance, "The 'classical' interval training program is running long distances with rhythmical changes of pace."

But I didn't like stopping during a run. I made it a point of pride never to stop. If I drank, it was on the run — running in place at water fountains if necessary. If I hit a red stoplight that couldn't be run because of traffic, I did laps around the lightpost. If my shoelaces came undone, I let them flap.

I didn't run fast but I always ran. I filled every hour with 60 honest minutes of running. I believed that stopping was for out-of-shape people. When you're fit, it only breaks your rhythm and cramps you up.

Ideas like this, if sound, stand up to the challenges of time and experience. There weren't enough challenges to change my thinking, but enough to make me wonder.

One person who made me wonder was Kenneth Crutchlow, an English adventurer. I talked with Ken in 1971 about a run he'd taken from Los Angeles to San Francisco. I asked him what kind of preparation he'd done.

"Oh," he said, "none at all. I wouldn't do any special training. That would take the sport out of it. The challenge for me was to do this totally unprepared — as any man on the street might."

"Yes, I see," I said. "But this is incredible. How can you run 50 miles a day for 10 straight days? Trained runners can't even do that kind of mileage."

"You want to know my secret? I don't hurry, and I don't run very far at one time — only a mile or so, and then I walk for awhile. Then I run some more and walk again. It takes the whole bloody day. But I get there."

Ken impressed me, but I rationalized, "His way is only for beginners. For them, rest breaks may be great, but I don't need them. I'm fit. I can run 50 miles straight. Why do I need to stop and walk?"

Walking was something I did when I was too tired to run any more. It symbolized pain and defeat. But as 1971 moved into 1972, running was increasingly painful and defeating.

Dr. Van Aaken warned, "The length of endurance (slow) distances in relation to tempo (fast) distances is between 20:1 and 30:1." That meant don't race more than 5% of the total. I ignored him, ran longer and raced 25% of my miles. This produced chronic exhaustion which set off a slow, crumbling breakdown.

I couldn't run 50 straight miles any more, or after awhile 26 miles, then 10, or finally anything until a surgeon fixed the self-inflicted damage.

After the cast came off and the stitches came out, I asked the surgeon, "When can I run again?"

He said, "Today. There's no reason to wait. The sooner the start, the sooner you'll see what you can and can't do. Just don't go very far. Go very slowly, and stop if you have any unusual pain."

I couldn't do much. That day, I set aside a half-hour and planned to run as much as I could, walking the rest. I ran only a minute of it. The next day, I ran a little more. Gradually, the amount of running grew and the walking shrunk, until after a few weeks I was running the whole way and thinking, "Great, I don't need the 'intervals' any more."

I again forgot Dr. Van Aaken's advice: "Run every day, slowly and with walking breaks." I thought it applied only to cripples.

PAUSES AND CURES

It's ironic that I only started paying attention to Van Aaken's ideas about playful intervals after I'd broken myself down with interval running. One kind hurt me, another promised a cure.

The hurting came in a bike-run relay. It was essentially a long interval workout: 2-3 minutes on the road, running hard; 2-3 minutes on the bike, recovering, when my partner ran. We did this for 12 miles — a dozen fast half-miles apiece.

My calf pulled on the sixth one, but I pushed on to the end. I could barely take a normal running step the next day, or the next two weeks.

About that time, Bill Rodgers won the Boston Marathon in record time. And he did it even after stopping once to tie his shoe, several more times for drinks.

At first, I thought, "Gee, look how much faster he would have gone if he hadn't taken those breaks. He would have been close to the world record."

He lost time with the stops, and lost some more by breaking rhythm. That's hard to pick up again after it's lost late in a race. You stiffen up almost as soon as you break stride. Or do you? By week's end, I would have by doubts.

The Friday after Boston, I was approaching normalcy again. I saw a neighbor running a block ahead that morning, wanted to say hi to him and made an interval-like spurt to catch up. A knifing pain cut at the calf muscle. I stopped and walked home, dejected, knowing I'd set myself back another 2-3 weeks with that dumb move.

Dr. Van Aaken came to visit that day. This was the first time I'd met the man I had been reading and writing about for almost as long as I'd been running. He had watched the Boston Marathon on Monday, and was now giving a series of talks on the West Coast.

Dr. Van Aaken ran through lots of topics in his talks. Interval running took up five minutes in more than eight hours of conversation and lectures.

He said what he'd been saying for years: "Run as a child runs. Run playfully, for 10 kilometers a day, without pain or fatigue. The plan is the same for everyone from competing athletes to men recovering from heart attacks. Only the pace and the amount of walking varies."

Van Aaken said his own children at play used "classical interval training." He told of following one boy when he was six years old. In two hours, he ran a total of about 10 kilometers — with some 400 pauses. And after all of this, he showed no fatigue. He could have gone all day.

Then the doctor moved on to the next topic. I would have missed the point one more time if I hadn't tried running long the next morning. It was the regular Saturday group run. I started jabbering away and forgot the sore calf as we headed up a long, gradual hill.

The calf wouldn't let me ignore it for long, though. Two miles out, another knife stabbed into it — worse than the one on Friday. I stopped and waved the others on, then swore and kicked at the ground for having to quit this run which is the highlight of every week.

My mood was ugly as I turned to walk back to the college parking lot. I brooded as I shuffled along. Then a half-mile down the road I realized, "Hey, that calf doesn't hurt so much now. I'll run for a minute and see what happens."

I ran and the muscle tightened, threatening to spasm again. I walked and it loosened, then ran again, a little farther than before, and walked and ran some more.

Back at the cars, I remembered I had to wait another two hours for my ride. "What the heck," I said. "I might as well be doing something with the time. If nothing else, I can walk."

I ended up going the full two hours, running about five minutes at a time and walking one.

All the way, long-buried nuggets of information were surfacing. I finally was seeing what Van Aaken meant by intervals . . . what "running playfully" is . . . how Ken Crutchlow was able to run 50 miles a day on no training . . . the reason I'd recovered so quickly from surgery . . . why Bill Rodgers' many stops at Boston last Monday may not have been so wrong.

My leg felt better after the two hours of run-walking than when I'd started. I couldn't have gone 2½ miles with steady running, but this way I'd gone five times that far.

Three days of "intervals" later, the calf soreness was completely gone. No injury had ever healed this fast. I could run all the way again, but didn't want to do it.

Short walking breaks along the way were so refreshing, I didn't feel like giving them up completely. And the running was enough faster because of the pauses that it easily made up for the few "lost" minutes. Even if the run took a few extra minutes, the time was worth taking if the pauses broke the steady upward spiral of fatigue, muscle tightness and pain.

And to think I needed only 15 years to reach the same conclusion Ernst Van Aaken had written in 1960: if you want to go long, you have to stop once in a while.

Harald Norpoth won an Olympic silver medal (5000 meters in 1964) and set a world record (2000 meters) while training with Van Aaken. The system included frequent walking breaks.

II
Training for the Future

In 1920, it was customary to train for the track distances by running a time-trial at one's racing distance about three times a week. Then Paavo Nurmi began to use forest runs plus fast repeat intervals over short distances of 200-400 meters (for example, 6 x 400m in 60 seconds) and this led to a powerful improvement in the best times of the day. With the Zatopek era, training distances increased to 20-50 kilometers per day at a slow pace (400m in 85-90 seconds) with rhythmically varied stress loads — 200-meter jogging breaks being inserted between intervals.

Later, Percy Cerutty of Australia, Arthur Lydiard of New Zealand, Jan Mulak of Poland and I all independently placed endurance conditioning by long, slow runs in the forest or on the roads at the center of running training (Herb Elliott's 48-kilometer road runs are one example), severely reducing both the number and intensity of interval runs because we recognized that in many cases intervals were superfluous.

I referred to optimal oxygen uptake capacity — acquired in a careful, reserve-sparing manner — as the alpha and omega of running training, even the basis of sprint training. At the same time sports doctors, especially the Germans, have to this day not been able to let go of the idea that it's necessary to practice oxygen debt, simply because it is encountered in races. Yet case histories have piled up of runners who have done long, slow distances almost daily and have improved their best times.

I'm so convinced of the value of endurance running that I imagine the training of the future for the 1500-meter runner who wants to run 3:20 but who'd also like to run a 12:45 5000 meters will include the following: 40 kilometers of running per day, preferably in five different outings spread over 18 hours. All running will be done playfully. The daily schedule will of course vary according to the individual's occupational or school activities. If, for example, the runner is a student and has five hours of classes and 2½-5 hours of studying or other activities, this is an example of how the training can be fit into his day:

5:45 — get up; run playfully 10 kilometers on road or trails. 7:00 — shower or bath; light breakfast. 8:00-1:00 — classes. 1:00-1:30 — five kilometers with easy accelerations, followed by a very small lunch and 15 minutes of rest, lying down. 2:15-3:30 — studying. 3:30-4:00 — five kilometer jog, closing with 2 x 500-meters at 1500-meter race pace. 4:00-5:15 — studying. 5:15-6:00 — personal time or reading. 6:00-7:30 — 10-kilometer run on roads, trails or track, finishing with 1000 meters at 70% effort and shower or bath; dinner to 8:00. 8:00-10:00 — studying or concert, theater, etc. 10:30-11:15 — 7-8 kilometer jog on the roads, followed by reading to 12 a.m.

This extremely concentrated schedule can be varied at will, perhaps being arranged even more effectively with just two or three training sessions per day.

On Saturday or Sunday, the runner might go out occasionally for 40, 50 or 60 kilometers with walking breaks, or as a continuous run, on roads or trails. The walking breaks can be in the form of 1-2 kilometers in race walking style, or the runner may wish to stop and do gymnastics exercises. One judges his level of effort during these runs by ascertaining whether he can maintain a continuous conversation with his companions. It's especially valuable to do an easy 500-meter acceleration every 10 kilometers and to put in 3-4 sprints of 60 meters occasionally, so as to include every racing style in one's long run.

ONE PRINCIPLE FOR ALL

Of course, the above training applies to the most talented and ambitious of runners. But a scaled-down version will be valuable to anyone. Let's take the case of a fun-runner between

18 and 80 years of age, whose racing distance is 10 kilometers.

Four times a week, jog 4-15 kilometers with walking breaks every 1000 meters if necessary. The pace, as usual, is one at which the runner can maintain a continuous conversation. At the end, do 1000 meters on a measured course at the race pace which is the runner's goal. Thus, an 80-year-old 10,000-meter runner who can still run 46 minutes will run 1000 meters in about 4:30.

The elite runner of the future will not train differently from anyone else — fun-runner, ambitious young middle- or long-distance runner, child, old man, woman. All running will be done playfully, in a state of respiratory balance. Even after several hours of running there should be enthusiasm and capacity for running faster.

A beginner of any age must be able to do at least five kilometers daily as soon as possible. To reach this level quickly, the runner must first insert many walking pauses into their runs, perhaps walking one minute after every 400 meters. In this way, even children six years of age or veteran runners taking up the sport for the first time at age 50 will immediately reach 5-10 kilometers per day in training. Even heart attack patients have been and are being trained this way.

Running training of the future will seek to increase the supply of oxygen to the cells, so that high average speeds can be maintained at all racing distances in a state of oxygen balance, right down to the final sprint which can then be initiated while the runner is completely fresh. The oxygen-using combustion processes in the organism create 20 times as much energy for the cells as does oxygen-less reduction of sugar in highest-stress interval training.

The most important principle for the runner of the future is that one learns to run by running. All peripheral exercises recede in importance unless they have an immediate effect on running style and endurance. For middle and long distance runners, therefore, weight lifting and strength training exercises which increase muscle strength with simultaneous increase in body weight should be limited.

With injuries or pains in knees, feet, shins, hips, etc., there should be no layoff. Rather, if it is impossible to run, bicycle training should be substituted. Training speed is individual but can be judged by one's pulse, which should not rise above 150. Total bicycling time should at least equal the time required for a normal running session. The basic principle is that stress is taken off the legs, yet they're never idle, and the circulatory system is kept working as long or longer than in running training. This has the advantage of continuing to train the endurance functions of heart and circulation while sparing one's reserves even more than is possible in running, where one's own body weight must be carried over the training course. No other sport is this complementary to running.

Running pace in endurance training is adjusted according to the person's individual endurance performance boundary, and only occasionally does he run at race pace. The relationship between endurance and tempo distances in training can be set at 20:1 — i.e., a person who's done 95 kilometers in endurance runs can do five kilometers of tempo runs, for example 7 x 700 meters, 10 x 500 meters, or 12 x 400 meters at no faster than race speed. A 15-minute 5000-meter runner will do 12 x 400 in 72 seconds at the fastest, with complete recovery during breaks of 200 meters walking and 400 meters jogging.

Tempo runs shorter than 400 meters should not be done by the long distance runner, because he has scarcely begun his tempo run and found his running rhythm when he has to stop again. On the other hand, the 800-meter runner who would like to run 2:00 can go ahead and run 4-8 x 200 meters in 30 seconds. But even he must recover completely during his recovery breaks and not explore his body's ability to withstand destructive testing.

FOR THE MARATHONER

The marathon runner has a special need for increased endurance training, because a person who wants to race 42 kilometers must very often have run at least that far in training, in order to accustom the organism, little by little, to this endurance stress load. Just as for example the 5000-meter runner very often runs longer than 20 kilometers in training, so must the marathoner gradually increase his training distance to 50, 60, or even 70 and 80 kilometers. Only in this way is the base gradually created for lasting 42 kilometers at race pace. These long distances cannot be run after a couple of years of training. Rather, it will take 3-5 years or more. If the runner is capable of such overdistances in training, then they should be repeated once a week year-round, and the runner should not shy away from an occasional ultra-marathon race.

A marathon runner can get along with two basic tempo variations:

1. 1000-meter runs at marathon race pace, repeated 20-42 times, or 1000 meters at the pace of the runner's personal best 10,000-meter time, repeated 5-10 times with long walking breaks.

2. Preferred are 2000- and 3000-meter tempo runs at 1½-2 minutes slower than one's best time, repeated 5-10 times. These should always be followed with the stimulus change of a few acceleration sprints of 60-80 meters at the close of the workout, so that every variation in style has been practiced in training.

The marathoner must on principle never in any phase of his training run encounter a significant oxygen dept. His pulse frequency must also not rise higher than 150 even at sharpest race pace. Otherwise, fatigue products will accumulate and from 30 kilometers on the race becomes slower and increasingly torturous. A well-trained runner of the future will increase his pace after the first half of race, and will finish with a long acceleration.

In order to force the reserves of liver and musculature to be built up out of the body's own substance — and to attain optimal running weight — occasional training days should be included on which the runner fasts. He will practice living solely from his reserves during training, even if he's running the marathon distance. Should his glycogen and carbohydrate reserves be used up, which is not to be feared in the case of a runner with five years of training behind him, the organism can learn in this way to switch over to the conversion of fat into carbohydrates — a critical point which signals the demise of many a marathon runner during the last third of the race.

Vitamin supplements can support the metabolism of the marathoner of the future. Particularly important are the vitamins of the B-complex, which are continually required in the respiratory chain of intracellular respiration and which are insufficiently present in the average diet of modern man — or rather, are destroyed by cooking. They can be taken in concentrated form as vitamin pills, or better, in the form of dried yeast, which contains all 13 groups of the B-vitamins. Vitamin C, on the other hand, is best gotten from lemons, oranges, or tomatoes, since it all too easily loses its potency in pill form. But one should not put too much trust in these things, because diet and vitamin pills don't make the runner. Training does. And the runner must not let diet interfere with running by eating too much or too soon before training and racing.

The runner of the future must above all relearn the art of fasting. He will run best with a certain feeling of hunger, because digestive work during a run is just so much energy wasted, diverting oxygen which is especially needed in peak performances.

SUMMARIZING

The Pure Endurance Method is based on a very few practical principles:

● Endurance training at the pace of optimal respiratory efficiency — at a pulse rate of 130 beats per minute — forms the basic training for all running distances from 400 meters up. Tempo runs at race pace and with few repetitions consititute merely a final "polish."

● Running is learned mainly by running; track running mostly by training on flat terrain and not by emphasized hill training, which brings into play different lever relationships in the working leg muscles than those used on the track.

● The biologically most important function in running training for middle and long distance specialists is endurance — defined as a composite of maximal oxygen uptake capacity, low body weight and economical application of structural lever relationships.

● Endurance is acquired mainly by prolonged exercise done at a moderate tempo. This tempo depends on the individual's personal upper endurance performance threshold. In training, this threshold is undercut by a few percentage points. Only occasionally is the actual racing pace practiced.

● Continuous training at faster than race pace, even for partial fractions of the racing distance is uneconomical and leads to depletion of reserves.

● Tempo runs are most effective when they're executed at the desired race pace, over fractions of the racing distance. The number of repetitions and breaks, and the length of the breaks depend on the individual's recovery ability.

● The meaning of the "interval principle" in running is to be able to cover more total mileage without fatigue, which is made possible by the rest breaks.

● All relatively intense anaerobic stresses (tempo runs) are prepared for by aerobic functions (easy runs), and followed by an aerobic warmdown jog.

● Avoid inactivity of your organism as you would avoid severe illness, and cultivate the endurance function as a pathway to biological durability.

Part 4

Children and Women

12

Running is Child's Play

In my opinion, one can't start this endurance training early enough in life, because, according to my observations, it is just children who are born long distance runners. What children do badly are such exertions as bicycling for speed, weight lifting and sprinting — particularly in excess of 100 meters. On the other hand, any healthy boy or girl is able to run 5000 meters at a moderate pace. The play of children is nothing more than a long distance run because in a couple of hours of play they cover many kilometers with several hundred pauses. The play of children is the primal form of interval training. Endurance training and a light bodily weight are prerequisites for good performances at distances over 800 meters. Results of my own investigations prove that the best long distance runners are those who have a great heart volume, a slight body-weight, and have strong and, if possible, long legs. The normal adult man has a heart volume of about 600 cubic centimeters. Sprinters, however, have for the most part also only 600-700 cc. Middle-distance runners have a heart volume of 750-900 cc., the long-distance men have volumes of 900-1200 cc.

If one divides the heart volume, expressed in cubic centimeters, by the body weight, stated in kilograms, the result is a quotient which I have termed the "endurance quotient" in German literature. In medical literature, this heart quotient may be regarded as the yardstick for determining whether the heart is too large or too small in proportion to the body weight. If the quotient is less than eight, then the heart is too small. If it is larger than 11, then, in the opinion of medical science, the heart is too large.

I myself have found that the best long-distance runners of the world show a quotient of 17, while very good — not the top — distance runners have at the very least a quotient between 12 and 14. The astonishing thing, though, is that children of 5-14 years of age whom I examined had much higher endurance quotients, on the average, than untrained adults. The reason for this is that in relation to their body weight children have a great heart capacity, especially if they are lively children.

I once examined a girl runner who was 12 years old and weighed 32 kilos. This child had a heart capacity of 435 cc., which gave her a resulting endurance quotient of 13.6 — a figure which only a good long-distance runner could show. In this quotient one can detect the relationship between a light body weight and the large beating capacity of the heart — or, to use a technical expression derived from the automobile, she had a strong "heart motor" and a light "car body."

This was no isolated incident. Sixteen other children, all of whom were under six years, showed similar values. The average heart volume of these little runners was 278 cc., their body weight was 19 kilos. Consequently, their endurance quotient was 14.6.

LONG, NOT FAST

It is an old-fashioned point of view to say that short-distance sprints of 50-100 yards represent a slight effort for a child, while long distance running is unwholesome because of the duration of the exercise.

Children can stay in motion for hours at a time while they play. In "keep-away" and other games, children run as far as three miles in an hour, with about 200 pauses. Once, I measured the total distance covered by a seven-year-old boy at play. He put in about 8½ kilometers in an hour and a half, with about 400 breaks. A healthy child can run and play all day long — strong evidence of the average child's health and performance capacity.

Coaches in sports clubs with age-group members know that children prefer distance running to sprinting. If they're not prevented from it, they'll run many kilometers while they talk, shout and hop around. To cite one example: a seven-year-old boy, a healthy child, came to me fresh from two hours of play in the swimming pool, and wanted to run 1500 meters. I encouraged him to go ahead, but to try 10,000 meters. That distance impressed him, so he set right to work. He ran 9600 meters at a steady, moderate pace, reacting to his friends' cries with cheerful answers and never out of breath. When he came to the final lap he was completely aware that this was the time for a spectacular finishing sprint. So he ran the last lap in 1:38 — six seconds faster than his previous best for that distance. He'd playfully run 10,000 meters in 58½ minutes. At the finish his pulse was 174, and after one minute his pulse rate had already fallen to 135. Since at this age a child has a pulse of 90 even while sleeping, and since his average pulse at play is around 110, his pulse frequency fall rate after a 10,000-meter run indicates faster recovery ability than is true of the world-class athlete.

A child reaches his normal pulse values in just a few minutes, because his organism immediately switches over to "play-pulse" levels after exertion, while the peak-class athlete's recovery time is considerably longer. The child is thus a born long distance runner, his play *is* running, and innumerable X-ray examinations have demonstrated that the heart of a child has a more favorable volume — relative to body weight — than an adult's. The more "grown-up" and heavy a youth becomes in terms of body weight, the less favorable is his power-to-weight ratio between heart volume (capacity) and body weight.

The youth of 16-18 must create for himself this favorable relationship by abundant endurance training. The healthy, playing child has it right from the start. Because of this fact, long-distance running at a moderate tempo (the longer the distance, of course, the slower the speed) is a natural for children. What these youngsters absolutely cannot endure is maximal running at 200 meters and longer distances, because this involves oxygen debt.

The observation is continually made that children who are sent off to run 400 meters start at full speed because of the apparent shortness of the distance, then because of oxygen debt they either fail to finish or wind up walking. But for playful running on forest paths, these same boys and girls between eight and 14 are virtually tireless.

Theory and practice are still diametrically opposed when it comes to training youthful runners. For example, following advice of Waldemar Gerschler of the Freiburg interval school, 14-18-year-olds were until recently allowed to run only the 100-, 200- and 300-meter distances, and 600-meter relays (this official German Track & Field Federation policy was established in 1948).

It has taken years of fighting in the German Federation (DLV) to get the 3000-meter distance approved for youngsters, and still affairs have progressed only so far that the older ones are occasionally allowed to run as far as 5000 meters.

The endurance capacity of the child and the adolescent are constantly being underestimated by both sports doctors and coaches, who still believe that short, fast running is the best stimulus to healthy growth. This is only true in a restricted sense — if the child runs playfully. But as soon as the stopwatch comes into the picture, all play ends. The youthful organism is then exposed to explosive muscle functions which cause oxygen debt, something the young body incurs with reluctance and which, if repeated too often, can survive only at the cost of organic damage.

What's true for the older runner is true also for children and adolescents: "Run daily, run slowly, run many miles, but at a speed at which you can hold a conversation."

HOURS OF PLAY

Children at play run tirelessly for hours on end, avoiding maximal exertion, and can run long distances at moderate pace without batting an eyelash. It is therefore incomprehensible why even today competitive distances for children of both sexes have been limited to the shorter races. Defenders of interval training think they've found support for their distance training theories in the child's play, with its long total distances and short recovery pauses. But they forget that the playing child runs no farther than 40-50 meters maximally, mostly shorter distances, during which the intensity of movement can't be compared with interval training's high stresses and shortest-possible recovery breaks. Since a child cannot incur oxygen debt, at least not to the extent that a trained adult can, it will choose to run its distance at a personally comfortable, easy pace and will rest when tired.

Sports medicine, which continually presumes to give directives for training on the basis of short experiments, was for decades in complete error when it came to judging the performance capacity of children in middle and long distance running. Let's look at just one example:

Two German sports doctors tested 10-year-old boys and 17-year-old teenagers on a bicycle ergometer, at the same performance level, for 10 minutes. The results were obvious: a 10-year-old simply can't match the "power performance" of a teenager. But the sports doctors had not considered that while an active 10-year-old boy, 4'6" tall, weighing 65 pounds can't produce the same power on an ergometer as a 17-year-old, he can run a middle distance like 1000 meters faster than the average untrained 17-year-old because of the younger child's favorable power-to-weight ratio.

Children simply are not the sprinters people have been trying to make them. As a consequence of their low body weight and slightly developed musculature, they are true endurance performers with relatively large hearts, the heart being a muscle which can be developed in boys and girls by the same training methods as are used by adults — contrary to an old prejudice of the sports doctors.

America, the land of sprinters and jumpers, has forged ahead to set a good example in age-group marathon running. Astonishing performances have been recorded, for example, by 10-year-old boys who've run under three hours; and by a girl, Mary Etta Boitano, who did 3:01 at that age. The Boitanos began fun-running when the children were quite young. One day the entire family, father and mother, six-year-old Mary Etta and eight-year-old Michael, jogged the marathon distance in 4:30. The children were far from exhausted, though it had been a great strain on the parents.

How can sports doctors document their hesitation with respect to children's marathoning, when such performances are now the order of the day all over the world? The marathon performances of school children speaks more eloquently on this topic than all the sports medicine studies of renowned institutes, which should refrain from giving guidelines for training but should attempt to theoretically document what's being discovered and confirmed in practice every day.

OMPhoto

13

Women are Built to Last

Johnny Weismuller, the Tarzan of numerous American films and a great swimming superstar of 1924-28, won the 400-meter freestyle at the 1924 Paris Olympic Games. His time was 5:04, and he was so exhausted at the finish that he had to be rescued from drowning.

A little American girl, 15-year-old Debbie Meyer, won the 1968 Olympic race at the same distance in 4:31. Despite the notorious altitude problem of Mexico City, Meyer was by no means as exhausted at the end of her race as was Weismuller. She also won the women's 800 meters in 9:24, a time which 10 years previous only a handful of male swimmers could equal.

The brute muscle strength of a well-built swimmer like Weismuller was insufficient for performances like those of the women at Mexico City, simply because not strength but endurance and technique are required for swimming long distances — two qualities in which the "weaker sex" excels.

The prejudicial stigma of "weaker sex" rests to some extent on an ancient Christian concept of woman's inferior mental and physical performance capacity. This prejudice was quite recently "confirmed" by sports doctors in performance tests which seem nonsensical to me. For example, female and male performances on bicycle ergometers were compared in various institutes. At the Institute for Work Physiology at Dortmund, results from hand-strength tests and similar procedures were compared, and men as a "muscle-type" were contrasted with women as the "weaker sex" in terms of muscle development — which is unquestionably true. But conclusions were drawn which devalued female performance capacity in all respects.

Woman is, however, because of her physical and psychic constitution, an endurance performer provided that the endurance stresses in question don't involve too-great muscle-strength demands. As far as I can tell, the absolute best endurance performance in swimming was done by a woman when Jenny Kammersgaad of Denmark swam a distance of 90 kilometers. That women are capable of significant endurance performances is proved by their results in hiking, mountain climbing, bicycling and running.

In track and field, women have had an especially hard time affirming their equal right to endurance performances. The 100 meters is still considered appropriate for women. But people don't consider that strength and sprint performances, as well as those in throwing and jumping, involve explosive muscle functions of which women aren't well suited as a result of their sex-determined inferior muscle development. But because of their lower weight and less-pronounced muscle development, and superiority to men in endurance and ability to suffer, women are predestined to be endurance performers.

In German track and field in 1953 and 1954, great arguments raged around the 800-meter distance for women. I was characterized in a large daily newspaper as an M.D. whose sense of professional responsibility and competence should be doubted — all because of my struggle to have the 800 meters accepted for women — a distance which is really still much too short. I was accused of wanting to breed "Zatopeks in pigtails." A newspaper writer recommended that stretchers, ambulance attendants and doctors be posted at the finish line of the 1954 national 800-meter championship event, ready to carry off the mortally exhausted women to the hospital.

After the preliminary heats, the same journalist did an about-face: "It was a wonderful image of grace and beauty, to see Marianne Weiss fly easily toward the finish during her final sprint." But 15 years had to pass before the German Federation decided to enter the women's 1500 meters and longer running distances in their program — innovations which had been suggested along with the 800 meters back in 1954.

All along, it was well known to many school teachers and other people who work with children that youngsters 8-12 years old can play for hours on end without tiring, and that girls of pre-puberty age are often superior to boys of the same age in running because of their thin bodies and low weight. Anni Pede of my Waldniel OSC club frequently ran the 12 kilometers from her home in Elmpt to Waldniel for training, when she was 15 years old, then ran 10 kilometers with her girlfriends, then went home again on foot. In 1967, after a four-year layoff during which she bore two children, she ran the marathon in 3:07:26 — then a world best.

Unfortunately, the entire thinking in women's training for track and field is still very much oriented toward the ideal of speed. Because of this, a well-known German trainer proposed at the national conference at Munich in 1969 that women candidates selected for national training courses intended for high-level performers should be able to run 8 x 200 meters in a very good time. This grotesque demand, a leftover from the folly of interval training's hectic stresses, is biologically unsound even for the strong male organism, while for a woman it's a sure path to biological ruin.

The unbiological demand for strength and speed as a basis for high-stress performance really brings the woman's "weakness" into sharp focus, namely her lower muscle-performance capacity. It represents a certain route to pathology.

However, the "weakness" of woman is her protection against overstress injury from explosive muscle functions, and is nature's prescription for endurance performance. The heart muscle is in any case not a "strength muscle" but a kind of endurance performance machine capable of about three billion movements in the course of a lifetime of 70-80 years.

The prejudice of sports doctors who — like many gynecologists — rarely have an opportunity to examine an endurance-trained woman, still refers to the "slight possibilities for coronary development" of women, though it's been proven by peak-class women's endurance performances that the heart muscle is the only muscle in a woman's body which can be trained to greater stroke power in the same way as it can in a man's. Anni Pede had a heart volume of 1040 cc., while the average untrained woman's heart volume is 620 cc., the untrained man's 730 cc.

Women will never have the strength and speed of men, and this is biologically completely unimportant because the durability of life depends solely on the endurance capacity of the organism.

Therefore, the question of whether women are the "weaker sex" must be answered in the affirmative if we choose muscular development as the criterion. But this is precisely an advantage for women in biological durability.

Woman's constitution is physiologically and psychically symbolized by the best endurance muscle in the human body, the heart.

THE ENDURING SEX

From statistics going back 100 years, we know that women are more enduring than men. For example, the average life expectancy of women is 73 years, that of men 69. In England, 20 men have birthdays of 100 years and over every year, compared with 100 women. Of 100,000 English female babies, 7.82 will reach 90, compared with 3.46 men.

The athletically most important difference between men and women is that 40% of a man's body mass is muscle, compared with only 23% for women. This limits women's strength and speed. On the other hand women have more subcutaneous fat, and thus have better energy reserves and protection from cold.

At 100-kilometer runs in Europe, women competitors have recorded better average times than many of the men. For example, Eva Westphal of Hamburg ran 100 kilometers in 10:11 at age 53, beating many men capable of 36-38 minutes at 10,000 meters, compared with Frau Westphal's 42-43 minutes.

In a 100-mile run (161 kilometers), American Natalie Cullimore (who'd previously recorded a best time of 16:11) won in 18 hours — ahead of all the men.

As mentioned, the only muscle which both men and women can train in equal measure is the heart. It was once asserted and supported with nice statistics that women have smaller hearts, but what was forgotten was that women have for hundreds of years lived in the seclusion of their household work.

The skeletal muscles of women work slowly and with endurance, like heart muscle tissue. Men's muscles are generally more suited to explosive functions at 100-800 meters. Men burn more carbohydrates in exercise, while women apparently use a higher relative amount of fatty acids and, perhaps, cholesterol.

Psychologically, men are more often explosive, inconstant, not enduring, and in pain and exertion — especially among high performance athletes — somewhat snivelling. Woman is the opposite: tough, constant, enduring, level and calm under endurance exertion and in the pain to which her biology exposes her (child-bearing). On the average, she is more patient than man. Armed with these advantages, women are in a position to do endurance feats previously considered impossible.

The first official women's marathon held was in 1973 at Waldniel, West Germany. Of 32 starters, 26 finished in good condition. It was obvious that most of the women suffered far less during the last 10 kilometers than the average man at the West German Championships. The winner, Christa Vahlensieck, who had trained from childhood for endurance, ran her first marathon in just under three hours. She had — in contrast with the men — a faster split for the second half of this long run, by nine minutes. Compared with her 10,000-meter best time, she ran 10,000-meter splits during her marathon which were comparable to those of Frank Shorter during his Munich marathon.

14

Women's Secret Weapon

by Joan Ullyot M.D.

A theory of Dr. Van Aaken is that women excel in endurance activity because of their fat metabolism. American doctor-marathoner Joan Ullyot, who speaks fluent German, interviewed Van Aaken on the subject, then explained it in this December 1974 Runner's World article.

Something very peculiar seems to be happening with women long distance runners. A few examples:

● Eileen Waters finishes her second 50-mile run at a pace of 6:30 per mile, running faster by then than any man on the track. And she isn't in pain like so many of the men. She crosses the finish line to set a new world record of six hours 55 minutes, smiles and exclaims, "Oh, I feel so great!"

● Miki Gorman, looking fresh after her victory (in 2:47) at the 1974 Boston marathon, says to the TV interviewer, "I can't run much faster, but I can run much, much farther. Once I ran 100 miles on the track." (The interviewer looks at 85-pound Miki in obvious disbelief.)

● Natalie Cullimore, in the 1973 Pacific AAU 100-mile championship, outlasts all the men in the field and wins in 18 hours — two hours slower than her best time but two hours faster than the only male finisher.

While I was having tea and chatting with Dr. Ernst Van Aaken, I mentioned these feats and wondered what was the secret of the women's extraordinary endurance.

The doctor answered immediately: "It's simple. They are running off of their fat."

This was a totally new concept to me (especially since, like many women runners, I am frequently dieting to get rid of fat). I eyed my apple-cake dubiously and ventured to ask, "But what about glycogen?"

Dr. Van Aaken laughed, "Is that why you are eating carbohydrates? All the glycogen you could possibly store would only last you for 30 kilometers (18.7 miles) at the most. A simple calculation shows that. All that apple-cake won't help you in a marathon. It will simply add to your weight."

Well, I finished my apple-cake without choking, but determined to find out more about fat metabolism in running. First, I conducted an informal poll of all the leading women marathoners gathered in Waldniel. None of them, surprisingly, had ever "hit the wall" in a long race. This unpleasant phenomenon apparently is far more common among men.

"Hitting the wall" is generally considered to result from glycogen depletion. Thus, various special carbohydrate-loading diets, designed to postpone the moment of truth by increasing glycogen stores, are in vogue. However, fat is always available as fuel, and perhaps women are better at utilizing it. (At present, this suggestion is purely theoretical.)

In the American and Scandinavian preoccupation with glycogen, the important role of fat has been overlooked. Fat in general is regarded as so much dead weight to carry about. Excess "depot fat" acquired by overeating is just that. However, must of the body's fat — especially that stored by trained long distance runners — is highly active metabolically and serves as a superior fuel for endurance performance.

Adipose tissue has a much higher energy yield per gram

Endurance-trained Christa Vahlensieck after her 2:40 marathon. With her (right) is Manfred Steffny, a German Olympian who runs by the Van Aaken method. (Noel Tamini photo)

than glycogen (7:1 ratio), is easily stored in the various nooks and crannies of the body, and in fact is preferentially – almost exclusively – burned by migrating birds and other species that must cover long distances. The principle endurance muscle of the human body – the heart – also burns fat in preference to all other substrates.

Classic experiments by Christensen and Hansen in 1939 showed that during *submaximal* (aerobic) work up to three hours, fat normally contributes as much as 70% of the energy requirement. The ratio of fat to carbohydrate used as fuel increases with longer exercise. Also, the proportion of fat used could be influenced by various manipulations – diet, workload and training being the most important.

In brief, glycogen utilization was highest in untrained men working closest to their maximum, and on a high-carbohydrate diet. Conversely, a mixed or high-fat diet, lower (aerobic) workload and, most importantly, long distance training increased the proportion of fat burned – up to 90%. In other words, the working endurance muscles became more like the heart.

Recent animal experiments by Holloszy in the U.S. have shown that training will almost double the amount of myoglobin, micochondrial (respiratory chain) enzymes, and the various enzymes involved in the breakdown and oxidation of fat within the leg muscles.

A Swiss researcher named Howald did muscle biopsies of well-trained male 100-kilometer runners and found an average of 22.3% fat mixed in with the lean leg muscle. This compared to about 10% in untrained men and in lean distance runners trained over shorter distances. (Fat contained *within* muscle is not to be confused with percentages of total body fat, which is low in all runners.)

The distinction between active, "trained-on" fat and passive, "eaten on" fat is very important. Only the former is useful. Otherwise, as Dr. Van Aaken points out, the best eater would be the best runner.

In order to develop the capacity to use one's fat

efficiently, he says, one should run daily over long distances (10-40 kilometers) almost always aerobically — slowly. Caloric intake should be limited to 2000 per day, including 50 grams of unsaturated fat, and runners should take regular fasts.

Granted that the oxidation of fats in running is much more important than most of us have realized. What does all this have to do with women? To begin with, even well-trained women usually have about 10% more fat than similarly trained men. Much of this fat is subcutaneous and serves as useful insulation.

More of the women's total body weight is stored fuel and correspondingly less is dead weight, i.e. muscle. Dr. Van Aaken emphasizes that the average woman is 23% muscle vs. 40% in men. In running, it is naturally important to be as light as possible — witness Miki Gorman — and muscular men are more handicapped than helped by their bulk over long distances.

In effect, then, women are built for distance running and will always do better, relative to their own capacities, where endurance rather than power is important.

Eileen Waters again provides an impressive example. In a 1972 marathon, she ran her best time of 3:03 (average of seven minutes per mile), starting out at 7:30 per mile and ending up at 6:30. Aside from the rather startling increase in speed with distance, this doesn't sound so remarkable . . . unless one knows that Eileen's best mile time is about 6:20. An equivalent performance by Frank Shorter would have him run 5:15 per mile for the first half of the race and finish at 4:15, averaging 4:45 for the whole run.

Eileen and probably other women obviously don't "run out of glycogen" and grind to a halt as so many men do. Two explanations are possible (and speculative):

1. Women not only contain more fat (fuel), but they know how to use it more efficiently. Possibly their enzyme systems are more geared to oxidize fat. As far as I know, all studies of fat vs. carbohydrate utilization have been confined to men — or male animals. It would be interesting to have some data on women — milers, marathoners and untrained.

2. Women may burn a higher percentage of fat, thus their available glycogen lasts longer and they feel better. This is quite possible even in the absence of sex-linked enzyme capabilities, since the more aerobically anyone runs, the higher the percentage of fat used. Glycogen seems to be reserved more for the anaerobic "heavy work." A man can easily run so fast that he uses up all his glycogen at twice the normal rate, and crashes early. By running aerobically, one can perhaps burn a better mixture of fuels.

Dr. Van Aaken defines the ideal long-distance runner as having a strong engine (heart) inside a light frame. The average woman will have a lighter frame than a man of the same height and an equally strong engine, since male and female hearts are equally responsive to training. But women may illustrate a third desireable characteristic: the ability to utilize "high-octane" fuel in the form of fat.

Part 5

Diet and Exercise

15

Diet for a Small Runner

Translated by Joan Ullyot M.D.

"All men and nations eat too much, and for this reason are not fit." This was the statement of 28-year-old Paavo Nurmi, the greatest distance runner of his time, when interviewed by the press during his tour of America in 1925. The young runner thus showed great insight into the standard-of-living situation which permits human fitness and health to waste away.

Mankind today, particularly in the so-called civilized countries, lives in a certain super-abundance. One can no longer speak of a "struggle for existence" as it was known after World War II. Nevertheless, the people in those days, especially in defeated Germany, were by and large far healthier than today's prosperous citizens. The German population after the war showed physiological findings which are found nowadays only in well-trained long-distance runners — namely, body weight about 10% below the so-called "normal"; low blood pressure on the order of 105/70; and resting pulse under 60. During the years of scanty food intake, 1945-48, the dazed population showed on the whole more endurance and physical fitness than present-day army recruits.

The billions of cells which make up the human organism need first of all a nutritional substance one could call the true "stuff of life" — oxygen. All other forms of nourishment are far less significant, though they nowadays are regarded, unjustifiably, as necessary to health. Everyone believes he can keep healthy by the proper diet. This erroneous idea is shared by doctors, nutritional experts and food faddists alike. They all believe that nutrition alone can enable a man to recover his health and to remain hale and hearty into a ripe old age. They do not realize that the digestion and metabolism of each and every kind of food ultimately requires oxygen.

A general formula for proper diet can never be found. The eating customs of each nation and people are too different, and what agrees with one can be harmful or at least disagreeable to another.

For instance, there are certain African tribes which delight in extracting long worms from under the bark of trees and slurping them up. Not only do they not become ill, they actually thrive on this diet. Missionaries report that the cannibals of New Guinea repeatedly urge them to taste human flesh, which they say is more delicious and nourishing than all other forms of meat. And who knows, perhaps the cannibals are right. Human flesh is not foreign to the human body, as are all other forms of meat!

The French take great pleasure in drinking wine, to the horror of ascetic-living sportsmen who abstain from all alcohol. The incredibly healthy Hunza people nourish themselves primarily with grains, apricots and yogurt. This diet, however, is not the reason for the good health of the Hunzas, but rather the hard living conditions which force these people to live frugally and toughens them.

The Eskimo is compelled to eat daily several pounds of walrus, fish and polar bear meat, and thus has a very unhealthy diet as far as his liver is concerned. However, the Eskimo has no choice in the matter. The Arctic milieu forces him to this way of life.

The rice diet of several hundred million Chinese is also not ideal, yet even under the hard living conditions of coolie laborers there were individuals of great endurance who could get by on 400 grams of rice daily. The rice-eating peoples were afflicted with beri-beri, so that there were always a certain number who died from lack of the essential B vitamin. But from the standpoint of dieticians who see salvation only in a well-balanced diet, these people should have been unable to live, much less multiply as they did.

Nutritionists as well as food faddists are forever specifying *what* one should eat. But it seems obvious that not the "what" but the "how much" is decisive. For with all food programs and recommendations of various schools of nutrition, one can eat oneself to death.

What one eats — the particular kind of diet, the countless nutritional admonitions — is unimportant. What is important is to keep the amount of food consumed to a minimum. By keeping the quantity of food low, the amount of oxygen required in its metabolism will also be low.

In order to burn one kilogram of fat, the body must utilize over 2000 liters of oxygen. So one must be extraordinarily active for long periods in order to get rid of excess fat and water through exercise. To keep the weight low, one should take in a minimum of food and a maximum of oxygen. The latter can be accomplished by virtually any kind of sport which is practiced daily at moderate intensity for prolonged periods. From the biological viewpoint, breathing contributes more to fitness and endurance than does eating.

NUTRITIONAL PRINCIPLES

1. Excessive amounts of food overload the digestive system and metabolism and increase the demands on liver and kidney.

2. A preference for sugar, white flour, and sweets will result in diminished intake of B vitamin. The immoderate intake of sweets impairs cellular metabolism (chiefly the process of oxidation) and results in lowered resistance to illness.

3. Excessive fat in the diet, especially of the saturated fatty acids (fats with a higher melting point) can lead to an overload of the liver and bilary system, with an increase in blood fats as well as an unfavorable composition of the important serum fatty acids. This results in an impairment of circulation, the danger of increased body weight and, ultimately, the promotion of arteriosclerosis.

4. In today's food, one must beware of chemical additives and also the residues of pesticides, and of the injections which are used in the breeding of certain animals such as chicken and beef. These substances can injure the cells, interfere with the enzymes necessary to normal cellular function, promote allergies, lead to storage of foreign substances in the liver, and interfere with the normal intestinal bacteria that are needed in digestion.

5. In order for food to have favorable effects and promote health, the amount eaten should be extremely scanty, the added salt reduced considerably below what is customary nowadays, and the diet should include plentiful amounts of fresh fruit and vegetables. The food value should be kept as high as possible. That is, the vitamin contents should not be reduced by excessive cooking or other processing.

6. The principal nutritional elements are carbohydrate, fat and protein, but the amounts recommended in earlier diets are certainly exaggerated, especially the amount of carbohydrate. Three hundred grams of carbohydrate, in the form of whole grain bread and similar products, are sufficient even for those engaged in heavy labor or sports training, if the diet includes about 80 grams of high-quality fat and 100 grams of protein. Milk and milk products are particularly good sources of protein.

7. Every person should select the foods he likes from among the many possibilities.

8. The most wholesome foods are those which only require a small amount of metabolic work for their digestion. Such foods include fresh fruits and juices, boiled or mashed potatoes and cream soups, skim milk and yogurt, soft-boiled eggs, and soft margarine (prepared without hardened fats).

9. Less wholesome foods, more difficult to digest, include smoked or pickled meats and fish, fried foods, mayonnaise, sardines, etc. One should avoid oversalted and spicy foods.

10. One could go on listing foods indefinitely. However, this would exaggerate the importance of these foods. Remem-

ber that it is not any particular diet which is restorative and health-giving, but the fact that one eats little of the diet. This is the basic rule which has been completely forgotten in the present day.

FIGHTING FAT

Even athletes are not exempt from excess body fat. Statistics for "normal" body weight are completely misleading. Ten percent under the published norms is better, and optimal weight for a distance runner is 20% under these figures.

Excess accumulation of depot fat in the cells is, in the final analysis, the cause of obesity. Certain cells are particularly inclined to fat storage, namely the fat-storage cells of the abdominal skin, the cheeks and, in women the hips and upper thighs.

General accumulation of body fat happens when food intake is greater than energy production in the form of work and heat. As long as a person is getting fatter or staying fat under his habitual diet, he is eating too much − regardless of how little it seems from his subjective point of view. Decreasing food intake to below what's necessary for current energy needs, leads inevitably to consumption of one's own body reserves.

There is, contrary to widespread misconception, no known inner disease, even of the glands, which leads inevitably to obesity. One nutritional scientist put it this way: "The only glands which play a role in obesity are the salivary and digestive glands."

If a person emphasizes carbohydrates in his diet, the excess is turned into fat. The organism acts as a depot for stored energy, since otherwise carbohydrates would be burned up too quickly. And so, while most carbohydrates enter metabolism via the detour of stored fat, the organism uses proteins and fat directly. A consequence of depot fat is water retention and excessive perspiration. At the same time, normal heat regulation is disturbed because of unfavorable surface-area-to-heat-production relationships.

To burn up one kilo of body fat requires 2000 liters of

oxygen, corresponding to walking 350 kilometers in 70 hours on running 120 kilometers in 16 hours. So it should be obvious that a daily one-hour stroll isn't the way to lose weight.

So what should we do? Since a person requires about 1700 calories even if he sleeps all day, a partial-fasting diet of 1000-1700 calories will certainly help, and will not deprive the body of important nutritional elements. A simple example of a seven-day diet would be:

Day 1 — five eggs eaten three hours apart; one liter of apple juice (1000 calories).

Day 2 — 500 grams of nonfat cottage cheese; 1500 grams of apples (1190 calories).

Day 3 — 300 grams of rice; tea (1100 calories).

Day 4 — 200 grams of veal cutlet; 200 grams whole wheat bread with 20 grams of butter; tea or coffee (850 calories).

Day 5 — one liter whole milk; one liter fruit juice (1140 calories).

Day 6 — 200 grams boiled potato; 200 grams whole wheat bread; one-half liter whole milk; 20 grams butter; 100 grams cheese (1680 calories).

Day 7 — 200 grams pork liver (steamed); 200 grams boiled potato; 20 grams butter; 100 grams salad; 100 grams tomato; one-half liter whole milk; one-half liter apple juice (1322 calories).

No one can gain weight on this diet, nor can anyone be deficient of important minerals, trace elements or vitamins. This diet also has the advantage of requiring little time for cooking, mixing, cutting, etc., and is easily prepared by any single person.

With daily endurance performance of any kind — as long as it leads to perspiration and lasts at least a half-hour and preferably is easy endurance running on roads or in the woods — a person following this diet will also promote eightfold increase in oxygen supply compared with sedentary work, thus burning off excess food. Aerobic exercise helps eliminate certain waste products and metabolic by-products from the organism via increased sweating and urine formation.

Having accomplished a 10-20% reduction of body weight below the so-called norm, the formerly fat person can return to his or her standard diet. Doing the seven-day diet three times will certainly take anyone a long way toward the goal of optimal weight. They should then see to it that they never exceed the caloric intake that allows them to hold their optimal weight. If they do slip and go beyond such a caloric threshold, they should switch back to the relative fasting diet.

"Don't eat like a pig" is the focus of Van Aaken's dietary advice. Obviously, Liane Winter doesn't, because she won the first world women's marathon championship in 1974 and Boston the following year. (Horst Muller photo)

16

Fuel for the Race

A trained athlete has larger supplies of sugar stored in his liver than the average person. This represents a reserve depot, in the form of glycogen. A person can run at least 100 kilometers on these reserves, as my nephew Jochen Gossenberger has proved. He fasted from the previous evening and lasted through a whole day of running on carbohydrate reserves. This is possible because fat can be converted to carbohydrate when necessary, and even proteins can be converted to glucose when the very last reserves of glucose, glycogen and fat have been used up.

It is ignorant to believe that a person who takes sugar just before or during a race has an advantage over the runner who doesn't. Were this true, running would be simply a matter of stuffing oneself full of carbohydrates. Thank God this isn't so. Performance ability is won by effort. A human being is not a machine, like a locomotive that you can feed on coal (carbohydrates) and expect good performances.

Marathon runners who learn to drain their carbohydrate supplies in training and then switch over to conversion of fatty acids are characterized by the fact that they can overcome the 20-mile "dead point" by a metabolic shift. A little bit of sugar — if possible with Vitamin C — is sufficient to set the changeover to fatty acids in motion. It is not, as many believe, the tiny amount of sugar that gives strength to run the last six miles.

Normal sugar supplies are not sufficient for running the

marathon. The glycogen stores in liver and muscles are continually supplemented by conversion of fatty acids and glucose. Training with a sugar deficiency can gradually urge the organism to build up greater reserves — similar to the way a certain degree of oxygen deficiency in altitude training causes myoglobin in the muscles to bind more oxygen. This is how world-class athletes run marathons at a continuous speed that would earlier have won 10,000-meter races.

Experience at the annual 100-kilometer run in Biel, Switzerland, shows that the ones who give up first are those who think they have to take food and drink all along the way.

When a decision must be made as to whether the muscles or digestive tract will receive blood while the body is doing work, the musculature inevitably wins. Thus, during strenuous physical work digestion is shunted onto a side track, if not actually stopped. Therefore, in high-level athletic performance, to eat is always a severe mistake, and can lead to cessation of movement — or at least to the simple solution of vomiting.

Even so-called athletic drinks, used in great cycle racing tours and running distances of marathon and greater length, serve no purpose of giving the body nutritional elements and calories. They only permit the utilization of body reserves, especially fat and glycogen, since the smallest amounts of sugar force the body to begin sugar metabolism processes. When sugar supplies are gone the body can immediately — if it's been trained to do so — switch over to fat metabolism for energy production. This happens in trained marathon runners usually at about 30-32 kilometers, where the runner must persevere until the body has begun to deliver sugar from the body's fat deposits, which the organism is able to convert into sugar.

Runs of 100 kilometers and walks of over 500 kilometers use up the entire stored carbohydrates in a few hours. These runners and walkers nevertheless survive, even running better if they've fasted for a day before the race.

According to the carbohydrate storage theory, Jochen Gossenberger should never have dared approach the starting line for a 100-kilometer run after a day's fast. But he ran without nutritional intake of any kind during the race, and from 70 kilometers on seemed as fresh as at the beginning of the race.

FLUID REPLACEMENT

While an adult metabolizes an average of 2.5 liters of liquids per day, the figure for an endurance athlete under certain conditions can reach 4-5 liters, so that the cells of the body are much more thoroughly irrigated and cleaned of debris and waste products which have entered the body from a polluted environment or from erroneous eating and drinking habits.

In the course of these hundreds of millions of years as fish evolved into amphibians and finally land animals, they brought sea water along with them — evolving also a distribution system with the heart as a pump, blood vessels and kidney as plumbing and filter. The kidney is daily irrigated by 1500 liters of sea-water-like liquid, the blood, from which it removes about 1.5 liters of urine.

The most important chemical in ocean water, as in human blood, is sodium, 98% of which is found in the spaces outside the cells and only 2% inside the cells. Potassium, though, is found 98% inside the cells and only 2% in the blood. Moderate endurance exercise maintains the necessary differences in concentration between the inside and outside of the cells, so that life and performance may flourish.

A severely decreased potassium content of the cells causes functional and structural cell damage, which can be seen frequently in overtrained athletes as reflected in sinking performance and an energetic heart weakness.

Certain other disturbances of the water and mineral balance should be known to the person who's involved in sports. For example, if there is insufficient blood or body fluid, the heart's blood-pumping work will be correspondingly decreased. The result is rapid heart beat, fatigue, nausea, sometimes vomiting, and — after exhausting athletic work — muscle cramps.

Sodium and salt loss is the real danger in marathon running

or in work done in great heat. This is called salt-deficiency syndrome, because more salt is eliminated than water. People who suffer from this situation look gray in the face, have severe vertigo and pressure pains in the head, are tired, walk wobbly, and in more severe cases lose consciousness. They should only be saved by being given salt solution, not glucose or circulatory stimulants. It is a mistake to drink too much water en route, thinning the body's salt supplies while for hours at a time eliminating concentrated salt solution through the sweat.

The endurance-trained athlete, and above all the marathon runner and the racing cyclist, must take more salt than normal, since a healthy, strong metabolism only functions optimally when sweat elimination and salt intake are balanced. I myself experienced the blessing of salt when, after amputation of the legs and the following fever of infection, I lay completely without appetite for three weeks, approaching death via rapid weight loss and dehydration. Oxtail soup, in small quantities for several days, awakened the spirits of life and appetite again. It stimulated the enzyme system and with it the metabolic processes necessary for life.

A marathoner stops for a drink during the German National Championship. Dr. Van Aaken says, however, "It is a mistake to drink too much water en route, thinning the body's salt supplies while for hours at a time eliminating concentrated salt solution through the sweat." (Rhein-Ruhr-Foto)

17

Two Ways to Warm Up

Since movement is the basic physiological stimulus for the muscles, joints and supportive tissues, gymnastics plays an important role in the maintenance of health. There are thousands of gymnastic variations, but a few basic exercises should be done every morning to protect the body and promote circulation for improvement of health, performance capacity and endurance. Here is one schedule:

Begin by brushing teeth and rinsing the mouth with plain water, gargle and wash face in cold water. Then have a two-minute hot bath with active trunk and leg exercise, and go on to the actual gymnastic exercises.

1. Arm circles forward and back with slightly bent knees. Or: spread legs and swing arms from outstretched position, forward between the legs and back, again. Or: in running position (feet about a hand's width apart and parallel) standing flat-footed, raise the arms to nearly perpendicular position, swing the trunk loosely forward while bending knees (arms follow through, down and back) and come back again to the starting position.

These first loosening-up exercises should be repeated between the other exercises.

2. From a forward trunk bend with arms stretched out to the sides (keep the trunk and spine straight and arms stretched straight out from the shoulders), turn the trunk alternately left and right.

3. In the position as described in number one, alternately lift a 3-4-kilogram object out to the side and forward to shoulder height, finishing by holding the weight in both hands in fixed outstretched position for a few seconds (isometric muscle strength exercise).

4. Jog lightly around the room or in place.

5. Do chinups on a bar high enough to keep the feet off the ground throughout. Failing this, try each day until you can do one, then several chinups.

6. Press a weight straight overhead with the help of leg muscles. Your goal should be to press your own body weight.

7. Lying on your back, arms next to the body, raise the outstretched legs to vertical position. Raise the outstretched legs about a hand's width above the ground, spread legs and alternately scissor-cross them. Raise to a shoulder stand (hands support the back) and loosely shake the legs; bicycle movement in the inverted position.

Raise outstretched legs (arms pressed against the ground) above the head, if possible, so toes touch the ground behind your head. Rock forward, lifting and bending the trunk and arms forward until the chin touches the knees.

8. Pushups — with straight back and also "cheater-style," bending at the waist.

9. Lying on stomach with arms stretched out in front, raise both arms, head and legs at the same time.

10. Running position — swing one leg forward and back, keeping arms relaxed and raised out to the side for balance. Switch legs, gradually increasing the arc of the leg's travel.

11. Forward trunk bend with feet together and legs straight. Gradually improve until fingertips and then palms can be brought all the way to the floor. At first you may have to make a few slight up-and-down movements to reach full extension.

12. From squat position with hands on the floor outside the knees, jump back into pushup position and back to squatting. This exercise is easier if you count rhythm: "one-and, two-and," etc.

13. Light hopping in place on both feet, or alternate three times on one foot, then three times on the other. The latter is easier if you again count rhythm: "One, two, three, and," etc.

14. Try a handstand against the wall or, if you can, a free-standing handstand.

15. Bend relaxed trunk forward and back. Let the arms hang down loosely, swaying slightly at both ends of the movement for a few seconds.

16. Trunk twist with outstretched arms and feet apart. Keep both feet flat on the ground so the trunk really gets a good twist.

The number of repetitions of any of these exercises depends on the individual's state of fitness. The cardinal rule is enthusiasm for movement, which ought to increase with regular practice. Morning exercises should never be torturous. After difficulty at the start, a person should always exercise within physiological limits defining joyful activity.

TAKE A HOT BATH

Certain uses of water and the direct application of heat to the body are among the most important ways of maintaining and increasing health. The surface of the human body is surrounded by air that conducts certain stimuli to the skin. Any decrease in area of the air/skin interface leads to specific changes.

Water pressure causes changes in pressure relationships within the body's tissues. For example, the backflow of blood and lymph vessels, which operate with low fluid pressure, is favorably influenced by external water pressure. Water pressure in a bathtub is greater than that in the large veins adjacent to the heart. Pressure in the chest cavity, and movements in the chest cavity, are also influenced favorably by bathtub water pressure, which stimulates activity in that part of the body. Water pressure causes changes in the body's blood volume which can increase the training effect in a healthy person.

Great differences exist in the heat exchanges that take

place when the body is surrounded by water. Water has 50 times greater heat conductivity than air, and water baths bring heat into the body or conduct it away much faster than air baths of the same temperature.

Hot tub baths are useful as a health-promoting aid, their effects being greater the longer and more deeply immersed a person bathes. Hot baths gradually increase the work of heart, circulatory system and the entire metabolism. A half-hour tub bath, especially if whirlpool equipment is used, is an extraordinarily valuable training method for the circulatory system. However, sauna and hot shower baths involve too much air contact to match the good effects of tub baths.

Swimming, so often exclusively prescribed by orthopedic specialists, is useful in most cases only at the very beginning of movement therapy. It is incapable of provoking the metabolic improvements which keep man, a land animal, optimally motion-competent and healthy.

All water treatment presupposes that the patient or person in training will warm up thoroughly beforehand and will rest afterward. The primary water treatment is swimming in water at a pleasant temperature up to 30 degrees centigrade. All exercises and free movements are made possible which, in the case of a crippled person, would not be possible without the buoyant force of the water. The combination of decreased weight through buoyancy and constant resistance of the water make movement baths particularly useful in the remobilization of injured muscle groups.

Ocean and open-air bathing belong likewise in the category of active baths, but their usually low temperatures represent a strong stimulus that not everyone can handle. Outdoor baths can only be generally recommended for those with normal heart and circulatory health.

Research shows that core temperatures of a thin person's body can sink as much as two degrees (C) after 10 minutes in cold water. Metabolism is accelerated by as much as 400% at the same time, so a quick dip in the ocean can represent a considerable stress. Since lowered temperatures were found in all test subjects even 80 minutes after immersion in cold ocean water, regardless of the thickness of the subject's subcutaneous fat, a person should normalize his lowered body temperature by a slow 10-minute run after bathing. Another recommendation is to do intense physical work while one is immersed in the ocean — for instance, fast swimming.

Thermal baths, on the other hand, do not lower the body's temperature and can therefore be used even in cases of impaired general health. The only active movement in a tub bath is raising and lowering one's trunk, perhaps bending forward at the same time — situps if the bathtub is large enough, or bent-knee situps if it is not. Situps are an excellent stomach-muscle and upper-thigh muscle exercise.

The favorable effects of hot immersion baths, though, come primarily from overheating and the heart stress it causes — in other words, from the training effect such baths exercise on the heart by raising pulse frequency, heart minute volume and oxygen consumption. In addition, body core temperature rises by several degrees. High core temperature like these can inhibit the development of most pathogenic bacteria and viruses, possibly even latent cancer cells. This effect may be theoretically explained as due to stimulation of defense functions.

While hot baths in general guarantee a certain activation of the total metabolism, localized hot baths promote limited circulatory stimulation. Foot baths or foot-and-ankle baths up to the knee demand high, narrow plastic vessels that hold 5-7 liters of water, to which is added a half-kilogram of kitchen salt. The temperature is raised as high as 50 degrees C, giving maximal irrigation in achilles tendinitis, torn ligaments, muscle tears, and other foot and lower leg injuries.

Alternating baths are valuable in the treatment of many running injuries. They are usually begun with a five-minute warm-water immersion, followed by cold-stimulus of only a few seconds. The warm-to-cold-to-warm process should be repeated several times, creating active expansion and contraction of the blood vessels.

18

Give Yourself a Break

Up to the Second World War, and even for a few years thereafter, it was considered proper after every competitive season to take a complete break, or a significant slow-down, or to do other kinds of sports for the purpose of recovery. Postponed operations and other health treatments were "caught up on" during the break, usually in the fall.

An ominous example of the "success" of this procedure is the case of Herbert Schade, many times German national champion at the longer distances. Schade had a tonsillectomy in the fall of 1953. I met him about two months later, and was surprised to see that he'd gained nearly 20 pounds. The specialist had emphatically warned him not to train for several months after the operation. This is a common occurrence when doctors who've had no contact with sports apply their experiences with ordinary patients to peak-class athletes. It is so very comfortable for the medical profession to give blanket prohibitions that convey the impression of wisdom and science, but which from an athletic point of view reflect only uncertainty and lack of knowledge relative to sports and its peculiar physiology.

A medical examination on Herbert Schade revealed how harmful total cessation of one's accustomed athletic and other daily activity can be. Schade was then holder of the German record at 5000 meters in 14:06, and at the time of his record had a heart volume of 1200 cc. After his layoff, he ran a test 5000, visibly straining, in 18:02, and his heart volume had shrunk to 890 cc. It took him months to get back into condition.

Training layoffs must therefore not extend so far that they lead to performance losses. Instead, after the competitive season the athlete should lay a base for future performances, or at least maintain his present condition, by doing judiciously planned training.

As we now know, preparatory training — whether in summer, fall or winter — must be arranged so that from one year to the next a regular progression of increases in health and performance is guaranteed — and so that any possible weaknesses of the muscles or errors in style can be compensated during this period. Fall and winter are the prime periods for rebuilding while resting the nervous system by avoidance of competition. The build-up period is a form of "active convalescence."

Actually, there are now no well-defined racing and off-season periods. The extent to which the boundaries between competitive and recuperative seasons can be erased is visible in Ron Clarke, unquestionably the world's best distance runner of the 1960's. Clarke was in top condition in both summer and winter, achieving his unusual consistency by running many kilometers daily at a speed that was comfortable for him. His example shows that regeneration after the competitive season can now be accomplished by continuation of the condition-building process in small steps and advances.

Clarke, whose build was really too heavy for an ideal distance runner, was only able to perform the way he did, year-in, year-out, because his day-to-day training was a constant process of building and recovery, and because readiness to perform well in competition year-round agreed with his temperament. But every athlete ought to build up his base during the recuperative period to such an extent that he will immediately be able to perform better at the season's beginning than his previous season's best times. (This is, of course, only valid for young athletes still in the process of building toward their career peak, whose potential is more or less predictable but whose path to those career highs will still take a matter of years.)

I've emphasized for decades now that there should be no yearly layoff in the sense of complete loafing, but that the athlete should seek recovery in joyful exertion.

Rehabilitation and regeneration do not take place under conditions of passive rest and abundant food intake, but in

Dr. Van Aaken: "There should be no such thing as sitting out cold, wet weather. You just have to protect yourself accordingly. . . If you change clothes immediately after running, there is no danger of catching cold." (John Cooper photo)

active recovery, "in the sweat of one's brow," without burning up reserves. This means that a stroll of even two hours' duration at a heart rate of 80-90 may not be enough, and exertions that drive the pulse up to 170 in unrelenting repetitions will, in the long run, be too much.

So how should a person, whether peak-class or plodder, train in the regeneration period after the competitive season?

REGENERATION PLAN

Start with an easy morning jog of 2-10 kilometers, depending on one's condition and ability. But one principle holds valid for all: early morning distance is run so slowly that one is actually just jogging along not much faster than walking pace, because the organism is not yet fully active.

Later in the day, the athlete may want to run 10-15 kilometers slowly enough that he can hold a conversation while running, and with walk breaks. If the runner feels increasing joy in running after the first few kilometers, he can go ahead and increase the tempo for 500-800 meters and do a few maximal accelerations of 50-60 meters without harm. This way, all running styles are practiced at least once a day. A peak-class marathoner can, of course, run up to 15 kilometers three times a day, but during the regenerative period he should always be running in a playful manner.

Young athletes in particular, who until a few years ago weren't considered capable of handling endurance exercise, and who in many countries are still confronted with "protective" rules affecting their competition distances, will find it hard to do too much in training provided they exercise at a moderate, playful pace. After all, a healthy child plays all day long.

In competition, on the other hand, physical and psychic overwork is the order of the day among both young and adult athletes. This can lead to all kinds of unusual symptoms and complaints. Training that takes a playful form, even during the competitive season, constantly regenerates the organism, while continuous repetition of near-maximal stresses in training and competition can become dangerous because of psychic stress effects and excessive demands on the circulatory system.

TRAINING COMPARISONS

Let's take an example from bicycle racing. Eighty races a season is not a very high average among road riders. Since places, not times, are what counts in bike racing, the weaker riders try to hang on without knowing how fast they're going. In cycling, there is no such thing as keeping track of one's performance capacity with a stopwatch. Thus, it's impossible to say whether Coppi or Anquetil or Merckx is a better rider than the cycling stars of earlier years. There are no universal standardized distances, as there are in long distance running. It would be absurd not to be able to tell who was better, Emil Zatopek or Ron Clarke. Yet in cycling this sort of comparison is unknown. Therefore, it is also harder to compare the value of training methods.

German cyclists and coaches don't understand that its riders train too little at a slow, rebuilding pace, and have decided in favor of wasteful methods, since earlier riders supposedly rode that way.

When, in 1966, the West German amateur racing cyclists once again finished near last place at the World Championships, it was said that the winning East Germans were "state-supported amateurs" who had a lot more time to train. In fact, the West German amateurs had just as much time, but the East German riders had put in 18,000 "playful" training kilometers during the off-season, while the West Germans prior had put only 4000 kilometers under their wheels in a frantic, strength-sapping effort to get into condition.

Arthur Lydiard, the successful New Zealand distance running coach, has written, "The sole and simplest kind of work for acquiring fitness is endurance exercise. The development of endurance alone produces the important condition of inexhaustibility or tirelessness in the body. For every kind of sport, as for life in general, a person needs endurance. And so it is very important for every coach or athlete to put great attention on the development of endurance before contemplating strenuous muscular exercises. The swimmer, the rower, the footballer — in fact, any athlete — should truly train 365 days a year, to keep himself fit for his sport. He should do a lot of running outside the playing season. In this way, he will maintain his endurance at the high level required in the exercise of his special sports discipline."

Lydiard's last sentences are particularly true for the cross-country skier, the long distance runner and the bicycle racer. In winter, it is almost impossible to train on the bicycle, and home "rollers" are ill-suited for the devoted racing cyclist's winter training. Basic endurance for all types of sports is acquired best by long distance running, because man is a "running animal" who either learns endurance running and playing as a child or remains undeveloped in his most important physical characteristic — movement.

Regeneration during and after the competitive season, as in daily life, occurs optimally when the body's oxygen-processing systems are in order. To burn off one kilogram of body fat, the human body requires 2000 liters of oxygen for combustion. In athletic terms, this corresponds to three marathons run in 2:40-3:00.

A daily stroll is by no means enough, even in the off-season, to maintain a high level of health and performance capacity. But processing an extra 240-260 liters of oxygen per day with 20 kilometers of running guarantees high-level fitness.

WINTER TRAINING

In earlier years, athletes used to take a break in the winter in order, they thought, to regenerate their strength. However, this we found to be valid only on a psychic level nowadays. If you're sick of running month after month on the road or the track, you should change athletic gears for a while, but by no means rest or get rusty. Getting rusty happens fast.

Emil Zatopek once said, "If I miss one day, I can tell that I'm several seconds slower." Famous pianist Arthur Rubenstein said of pauses in practice, "When I take a day off, I notice it. When I miss two days, the audience notices it." And so it is with running training.

There should be no such thing as sitting out cold, wet weather. You just have to protect yourself accordingly. Obviously, you don't have to work for maximal hardness and natureboy exhibitionism. Just dress warmly to conserve energy. In very cold weather, hands and face must always be protected. Running shoes should be waterproof or coated with water repellent.

Even in great cold, distance runs in winter have to lead to perspiration — not because of running speed but because of the length of the runs. This slow heating of one's own inner oven strengthens the runner's resistance. If you change clothes immediately after running, there's no danger of catching cold. Even when you don't feel quite right or have a mild fever, distance running in winter can accelerate a cure.

During very cold weather, only run as many miles as you can while staying comfortably warm and reasonably dry. There should be no more effort to force more miles out of yourself in winter than in summer. You can always make it up in March and April during the early good weather.

Though winter training consists of slow runs and perhaps less miles than in fall or spring, it is done daily, regardless of the weather. Winter training should strengthen the heart, increasing oxygen uptake capacity and keeping the circulation tuned. This is true for sprinters as well as distance runners. It's best to do long runs all winter long, finishing the season with gradually increased tempo runs (maximum length of 700-1000 meters at 70% of top speed).

Every long run can be followed by just one tempo run a day, or a few submaximal accelerations of 60 meters or so. This way, you will be sure to have practiced all the possible variations of tempo from warmup to sprint, and you won't have to go through a radical change at the end of the winter.

The runner should be ready to race at any time on this base training, but actually he should only race playfully and without any great attachment to results — just to test his form or learn tactics. The most important thing is for the runner to very seldom give his all during winter.

Muscles are best irrigated by slow running and a heart rate of 130-150. The running muscles require formation during the winter of a great number of fine, hair-like blood vessels to insure a better blood supply. The runner has to make his body an oxygen supermarket in winter, and avoid excessive consumption of energy in oxygenless (anerobic) reactions.

In winter, it comes right down to the vital stuff of life, oxygen. In summer competition, you can occasionally overdraw your account and incur an oxygen debt. You survive these overdrafts better when you have a nice, fat oxygen account.

Part 6

Questions and Answers

19
Final Analysis

by Tom Sturak

Tom Sturak's late-1974 interview with Dr. Van Aaken went a long way toward clarifying false impressions about his method among English-speaking readers. It was published in January 1975 Runner's World.

You told me before the interview that your motto is "run long, run daily, drink little and don't eat like a pig . . ."

My whole teaching in one sentence is "run slowly, run daily, drink moderately and don't eat like a pig."

Everything we have heard — and I'm sure a lot of what we've heard has been distorted — has been that a runner should be almost emaciated. I'm wondering if Harald Norpoth (6'2", 130-pound former world record holder, coached by Van Aaken) is indeed your "ideal runner."

The most important thing is the weight. In the future, it'll be the person who has a large heart and the least weight who does best. It doesn't matter so much how much is muscle and how much is fat. It's mainly a matter of weight. Everybody is trainable. Everybody can bring their weight down, and everybody can train their heart. So everybody can bring themselves closer to this ideal.

Ernst Van Aaken at 50—former pole vaulter, marathon veteran and a growing authority on endurance training—races 4:41 for 1500 meters.

You have said, look at the "ideal" weight charts and get 20% below this. Steve Prefontaine for one criticized this, saying he has big bones and could never get down to that. He'd be so weak he couldn't run.

If you take two men of exactly the same height, one a shot putter, and the other Harald Norpoth, and you weigh the bones, the difference in the weight of the bones is only going to be 900 grams (about two pounds). The normal weight is a function of the muscles, the water and the connective tissues.

Would you have advised a big-boned heavily muscled runner like Prefontaine to lose weight?

He probably couldn't have brought his weight down further, any more than Norpoth could bring his weight down further. Every person has his own weight where he has gotten rid of practically all of the fat. He can't get down lower than that.

I'm quite sure that Norpoth has a larger heart than Prefontaine and he (Norpoth) has better leverage in his arms and legs because they're longer. Prefontaine was smaller. He ran 13:20 for 5000 meters, which Norpoth also has run. But Norpoth has the potential to run under 13 minutes.

Filbert Bayi, incidentally, is exactly the same height and weight as Norpoth. Lasse Viren also has the same build, and showed what he could do with it in Munich (where he won the 5000 and 10,000 meters).

Keeping light, then, is one of your principles. Another is to run slowly. How slowly?

With Harald Norpoth, I had to teach him to run slowly. By "slowly," I mean 400 meters in two minutes (about eight-minute mile pace). He'd do it 10 times, 4000 meters total, as a start. This would be 350 meters of running, a minute of walking, again slowly 350 meters, etc. Of course, this training could last for 10 hours . . .

That's the other question. If you're going to have that low quality, then how much quantity would a runner do? Surely Norpoth did more than 10 times 400 meters.

Van Aaken, wearing an Oregon Road Runners Club t-shirt, is interviewed by Tom Sturak (who took this photo) at the doctor's home in Waldniel.

After he ran the 10 rounds of 400 meters, he ran 2000 meters — one minute slower than his best time. His best was five minutes, so he ran six minutes. Then he did 10 more slow 400-meter runs, then another 2000, and on and on until he ran 17 or 18 kilometers.

Even the little children in Waldniel run that way, 10 kilometers a day. After one little girl of six had done this for half a year, she ran 5000 meters in 22 minutes. Many of the older runners in Germany have also started this way.

What's important to note here is that Norpoth ran 2000 meters in six minutes. Now that's not bad! That's quality running for a workout. Apparently we've had the misconception that you never use fast training.

We have a misconception of interval training. The founder of "intervals" was Hannes Kolehmainen of Finland (1912 Olympic champion). But that wasn't interval training as we now know it. Kolehmainen said, "Why should I run 10,000 meters in one stretch? I can run 1000 meters 10 times." He improved greatly when, in addition to his long runs of 30 kilometers, he did one-kilometer runs in 3:20. It's wrong to call these intervals runs. They were "tempo" runs with long pauses in between. He improved with them from 15:10 to 14:36 for 5000 meters.

Then came Paavo Nurmi. He ran every day, 10-20 kilometers in the woods. And then several times a week he would run 6 x 400 meters in 60 seconds.

But isn't that anaerobic running?
Yes, anaerobic.

So you're not against anaerobic running in training?
I'm only talking about history. We haven't come to my own ideas yet. Most people don't know the roots of this kind of running.

Nurmi's success was based on the fact that he ran more kilometers than Kolehmainen, and he ran harder tempo runs. He ran only a few seconds faster for 5000 meters, but almost two minutes faster for 10,000 meters.

Next in the history of long distance running came Emil

Zatopek. He told me his main training was to run 60-100 x 400 meters, each in 1:36 (about 6½-minute mile pace). That's the tempo of a 20-minute 5000-meter run. He never stopped. He just interrupted the runs with 200 meters of very slow jogging.

We shouldn't call these intervals because people will think they were fast. He would run 60 x 40 meters jogging and 60 x 200 meters *less than jogging*. He did this every day. It amounted to 36-50 kilometers, slowly. Occasionally, he would run 30 x 300 meters in 46 seconds. Zatopek ran 10,000 meters more than a minute faster than Nurmi.

Then everybody misunderstood what Zatopek was doing. For instance, here in Germany they said, okay, we're going to run 200 meters very fast with very short pauses. Everything in Germany went *kaput*. Performances went down. This type of interval training went like a plague throughout the world.

When did you realize that something was wrong with this fast interval training?

In 1947, I wrote that in order to run 1:40 for the 800 meters, a runner must be able to run the 400 in 46 seconds but also must train like a marathon runner. This would give a synthesis of endurance and speed.

In 1955, I said that one probably doesn't have to do any tempo runs at all. What counted with Zatopek was the number of kilometers he ran. One should run a high number of kilometers where the pulse is between 130 and at most 150 . . .

Let me interrupt. When Norpoth is running 2000 meters in six minutes, his pulse isn't going to go above 150?

When I talk about those 2000-meter tempo runs, that's the second or third level of training. Most important is the ground or base training, where for months and even years you do long training so as to build up your ability to use oxygen. Anyone can do the basic training — man, woman, child, old person — and it can only do them good.

How much training should one do?

A minimum of 10 kilometers a day, even for children.

Former world record holders Franz-Josef Kemper (second from right) and Harald Norpoth (right) on a long and easy-paced winter training run in Germany. (Horst Muller photo)

We've read that you think a marathon runner should do the equivalent of the marathon distance each day. Is this figure accurate?

Forty-two kilometers (26 miles) is fine, but there are those like Gaston Roelants of Belgium who have trained up to 80 kilometers (50 miles) a day. But his legs couldn't bear this.

But there are others like Jack Foster who told me personally that he never runs more than 70 miles a week and sometimes as little as 35. Yet at age 42, he can run under 2:15 . . .

Yes. And Eva Westphal, a 56-year-old German 100-kilometer runner, never has time to train more than five or 10 kilometers a day.

And so what does all of this mean — that runners may not need as much quantity as you suggest?

When we see what Jack Foster does at his age, then we can say if someone who is 25, built like Norpoth and trained like Roelants (without injuries), he would run the marathon in 1:55. We are just at the beginning. In 1936 at the Berlin Olympics, they thought that 2:29 would be the limit. Now we have several hundred in the world under 2:20.

In training, do you ever advise all-out running of any sort? Is it necessary to "race the heart" occasionally?

An example is Maria Strickling. She ran interval-type training for 10 years, and her best time was 2:20 for the 800. Then she began the long training, and at the end of every 12-kilometer run she would do 6-8 x 60 meters — not all-out but very fast. She improved her 800 time to 2:06, and her 100 time from 13.4 to 12.5.

Norpoth learned that after running 15 kilometers in the woods, he had to run 3-5 x 500 meters, never faster than 80 seconds. A little bit of fast training seems to be enough.

You talked earlier about the importance of low weight. Can you describe in more detail your recommendations on diet?

The scientists say that a man needs 1700 calories a day and a woman 1500 just to sleep all day, maybe 3000 if they work. This is all nonsense. During the war and just after, the German population as a whole was only eating 800-1000 calories a day. And there were almost no heart attacks despite tremendous stresses from bombing, losing their homes and families, etc.

Now we have more than 150,000 deaths from heart attack each year in Germany. This rise in heart disease has paralleled the rise in food consumption. So my conclusion from this is that it doesn't matter so much what you eat, only that you eat very little. If you eat moderately with a balanced diet, you cannot lack for vitamins, minerals and trace elements. You keep the weight down if you just control the quantity.

If you're just sitting here, you're using about one-fourth liter of oxygen per minute. If you're walking, you use about a half-liter. But if you run at a pace at which you can converse, you use two liters — eight times as much as if you were sitting.

From that comes the basic rule of training, which is eat little and get lots of oxygen. To burn one kilogram of fat, you have to use 2000 liters of oxygen to do it. A 2:30 marathon uses 500 liters of oxygen, so you need to run four marathons to lose one kilo of fat. Therefore, running is not the way to lose weight. You have to fast.

What do you mean by "fast"?

Eat only 1000 calories a day if you want to lose weight. Train when hungry so the body learns to switch over to burning fat instead of carbohydrate. Run at least 14 hours after eating. If you can teach the body to shift gears this way, you can run 500 kilometers (300-plus miles).

What are your views on carbohydrate-loading before a race?

It doesn't do much good. The most glycogen you can ever load is 600 grams, and that's enough for only about 30-35 kilometers. Then you have to switch over to burning fat.

If one has the idea that through eating and drinking he can become a better runner, this is practically and physiologically unproven. What is important is the oxygen you use. You use oxygen by running slowly, 10-20 kilometers daily. To be healthy, you must train — and eat — like a marathoner.

20

A Success Story

by Joe Henderson

The Meinrad Nagele of today bears little resemblance to the one who occupied the same, considerably more bulky body less than 10 years ago. Overindulgence in fruits of prosperous post-war West German living and the pressures of his work as a traffic expert were telling. He was only 37, not old. But his frame was carrying 212 pounds—none too gracefully—and he was constantly trooping off to his doctor to have his circulatory complaints cared for.

Now we flash ahead nine years to May 1970. The same Meinrad Nagele, dozens of kilograms lighter and obviously healthy, had just completed the World Veterans' marathon run in Sweden. More than just completed it, actually. He finished fourth—first among men over 45—in a time that aroused envy among marathoners half his age. 2:29:45.

Nagele's saga of his trip from fat 37-year-old to fast 46-year-old is an incredible as the story of the method that took him there. He got his inspiration from Ernst Van Aaken.

After his race in Sweden, Nagele wrote, "The vast improvement I attribute to endurance training carried out consistently over a period of many years, together with a special diet (involving natural foods and fasting). This combination is the only method guaranteed to permit acquisition of the highest possible endurance potential.

"For example, on the 20 days prior to May 11 (the race was on May 17), I ran 25 miles per day. In the morning, about

11 miles at nine minutes per mile and in the evening about 14 miles at 8½-minute pace."

He'd come a long ways in nine years. Al Guth of the Los Angeles Senior Track Club, a personal friend of Nagele, tells of the West German's running beginnings in 1961:

"That year he joined a 'senior gymnastic group,' sweated off about 35 pounds and earned a Sports Badge (a popular all-around track and field test in West Germany, consisting of five events; his performances included 20:39 for 5000 meters). An instructor advised him to try distances and—in spite of his age—to use interval training to improve his speed. Using work-outs such as 10-15 x 200 meters in 30-32 seconds with 200-meter breaks, he was able to get down to 10:46 for 3000 meters. But he suffered from insomnia, nervous irritation, and also more and more lacked the will to train."

Meinrad quit running in favor of shot putting. His weight shot back up over 200 pounds, and his health wasn't improving noticably. Then he stumbled onto the Van Aaken method. The doctor advised him to start with slow runs—five miles, three or four times a week. By spring, with slightly longer slow runs and a few repetitions (10 x 500 meters in 1:40 with 200-meter walking breaks), all his times improved markedly. At age 39, weighing 145 pounds by now, and less than a year after adopting the endurance method, he was running 800 meters in 2:04.9 and 3000 in 9:31.

"In 1964," Guth writes, "Meinrad survived his first marathon in 3:19, but three months later he ran 3:02. By 1967, he was down to 2:37, plus 15:41 for 5000 meters and 32:23 for 10,000. This was at age 43."

Then, Nagele began experimenting with what he called "super-endurance training." He ran 30-45 miles every Saturday

Shortly before the accident which cost him his legs, Van Aaken trained with Meinrad Nagele (left), co-founder with the doctor of the Association of Veteran Long Distance Runners.

at very slow pace—about nine minutes per mile. Guth relates that this "enabled him to run for hours without noticeable effort. For two years, he trained twice daily, and thereby reached 30-35 kilometers every day."

Any distance coach is made famous by his runners as often as he makes the runners famous. It's world records and Olympic championships that draw attention to coaching methods and the men behind them. Van Aaken hasn't be too involved with— or even too concerned with—spectacular racing successes; though men like Harald Norpoth have achieved them. The doctor is more concerned with reclaiming health through running. And perhaps in this sense Meinrad Nagele is more successful than any Olympic medalist.

INDEX

ABOUT THE AUTHOR

Ernst Van Aaken was born May 16, 1910, in Emmerlich, Germany. During the 1930s, he studied astronomy and physics, but later switched to medicine.

Dr. Van Aaken served during World War II as a surgeon and director of a field hospital. Then after the war he set up his medical practice in the village of Waldniel. That same year, he began writing about the "pure endurance method" which he had been formulating since the 1920s—after he'd watched Paavo Nurmi in the Olympic Games.

For many years, Van Aaken combined running, gymnastics and pole vaulting. He vaulted 11'6" and finished his first marathon at the age of 40. Ten years later, he ran 4:41 for 1500 meters.

He founded and coached of OSC (Olympic Sports Club) Waldniel, and in 1960 set up the German Association of Veteran Long Distance Runners. The Association became worldwide in the mid-'60s, with Van Aaken and Meinrad Nagele being the guiding forces.

Van Aaken continued running until 1972, when on a rainy evening he was struck by an auto while training. Both legs were amputated below the knees.

The German version of this book, *Programmed for 100 Years,* was published a short time later.